Marketing Mix Decisions: New Perspectives and Practices

MARKETING MIX DECISIONS: NEW PERSPECTIVES AND PRACTICES

Editors
Roger A. Kerin
Rob O'Regan

Chicago, Illinois

Library of Congress Cataloging-in-Publication Data

Marketing mix decisions : new perspectives and practices / editors Roger A.
Kerin, Rob O'Regan.
    p. cm.
  Includes bibliographical references and index.
  ISBN 0-87757-330-1
  1. Marketing--Decision making. 2. Marketing--Management. 3.
Marketing--Costs. I. Kerin, Roger A. II. O'Regan, Rob, 1961-

  HF5415.135.M374 2008
  658.8--dc22

                              2008015404

American Marketing Association
311 S. Wacker Dr., Suite 5800
Chicago, IL 60606

Composed by Sarah Burkhart
Cover design by The Glasoe Group

This book is printed on acid-free paper.

Printed in the United States of America

CONTENTS

FOREWORD

The Board of Directors of the American Marketing Association formed a coalition of top academics and senior marketing executives to drive the development and dissemination of marketing knowledge that will help marketing management address key challenges and opportunities in the marketplace.

The Knowledge Coalition's first action was to conduct interviews with high-level marketers at business-to-business and business-to-consumer companies in various industries to determine their most important information and knowledge needs. Consistent responses across the interviews were that the top issue was resource allocation and marketing mix planning resulting from shifts in customer/consumer attitudes and behavior due primarily to the advances in technology and the proliferation of media and channels.

The American Marketing Association is pleased to present this book, which addresses the challenge of marketing mix decisions. It is the first offering in our new Marketing Knowledge Series from the Coalition. Additional information and learning on this topic will be released, and knowledge on other topics will also be developed and disseminated by the Knowledge Coalition.

Our sincere thanks to the volunteers who have been involved in this effort, particularly the original and current cochairs of the Knowledge Coalition:

Robert F. Lusch
Professor of Marketing
University of Arizona

Michael J. Houston
Ecolab-Grieve Chair,
  International Marketing
University of Minnesota

Mike Winkler
Retired Executive Vice President
CMO
Hewlett-Packard

Jeff Hunter
Director, Consumer Insights
General Mills Inc.

Thanks also to the coeditors of this book, Roger A. Kerin, Harold C. Simmons Distinguished Professor of Marketing at Southern Methodist University, and Rob O'Regan, Principal at 822 Media, LLC.

Dennis Dunlap
Chief Executive Officer
American Marketing Association

ACKNOWLEDGMENTS

Numerous individuals deserve recognition for the book's initiation and development. They include the American Marketing Association Board of Directors, American Marketing Association Knowledge Coalition Members, authors, and reviewers.

Members of the AMA Knowledge Coalition were and remain actively engaged in identifying significant topics that have the potential to advance both marketing theory and practice. Past and present members of the AMA Knowledge Coalition include the following, in alphabetical order:

Rajesh Chandy
University of Minnesota

Patrick T. Crane
Eastman Kodak Company

William Cron
Texas Christian University

Dennis Dunlap
American Marketing Association

Thomas K. Hernquist
The Hershey Company

Michael J. Houston
University of Minnesota

Jeff Hunter
General Mills Inc.

Kevin L. Keller
Dartmouth College

Michael E. Kullman
DuPont

V. Kumar
University of Connecticut

Robert P. Leone
Ohio State University

Robert F. Lusch
University of Arizona

Richard J. Lutz
University of Florida

Deborah J. MacInnis
University of Southern California

H. Paul Root
Marketing Science Institute

Fred Webster
University of Arizona

Mike Winkler
Hewlett-Packard

Valarie Zeithaml
University of North Carolina

Gordon Wyner
Millward Brown Inc.

This volume was made possible by the seven contributing authors. Each author has written or collaborated on an original article for the book and labored through a rigorous review process. The authors are listed alphabetically, as follows:

Sunil Gupta
Edward W. Carter Professor of
  Business Administration
Harvard Business School

Venkatesh Shankar
Coleman Chair in Marketing
Texas A&M University

V. Kumar
ING Chair Professor in Marketing
University of Connecticut

Thomas J. Steenburgh
Assistant Professor of Marketing
Harvard Business School

Anil Menon
Vice President, Marketing &
  Strategy
IBM Systems & Technology
  Group

Gordon Wyner
Executive Vice President of North
  American Strategy
Millward Brown

Todd M. Powers
Director, Brand Research
IBM Market Intelligence Center
  of Excellence

Many people also participated in the review process at different stages of manuscript development. Knowledge Coalition members provided suggestions for topical coverage and comments on manuscripts. Special thanks are due to William Dillon, Southern Methodist University; Rajdeep Grewal, Pennsylvania State University; Donald Lehmann, Columbia University; Robert Leone, Ohio State University; and H. Paul Root, Marketing Science Institute, for their willingness to assume a heavier reviewing load.

Roger A. Kerin, Southern Methodist University
Rob O'Regan, 822 Media, LLC

INTRODUCTION

Marketing Mix Resource Allocation and Planning Challenges

Marketing mix resource allocation and planning has assumed prominence as companies have attempted to optimize spending across all marketing activities. That's no surprise, considering that senior marketing executives are under increasing pressure to help their organizations achieve organic sales growth with tighter, top-down-driven budgets and short time horizons to deliver tangible payback on their marketing campaigns. With less influence over the size of their budgets, senior marketers must instead attempt to maximize the impact of the dollars they distribute for programs across multiple products, markets, channels, and specific customers, using an increasingly complex mix of new and traditional media.

As a result, companies have looked toward analytical and modeling techniques in an attempt to better link marketing investments to meaningful and measurable market responses (and, ideally, to one or more financial metrics). Packaged goods and pharmaceutical marketers, in particular, were among the pioneers in exploring marketing mix analytics and data-driven econometric models. Marketing scholars also have contributed to a more sophisticated body of analytical and modeling literature that offers both theoretical and substantive insights for marketing mix resource allocation decisions and planning practices. In many respects, marketing practitioners and researchers were early advocates for bringing analytics to business practice (Kotler 1971).

Nevertheless, changing customer dynamics and advances in media technology present novel challenges. Nowhere is the challenge more evident than in the domain of new media that originated in and is energized by the digital environment. The rapid and ongoing emergence of new digital channels—from the static online banner ads of the 1990s to the social media and mobile platforms of the current environment—has changed the way people consume information and has left marketers scrambling to address the new digital landscape. According to a recent report by Booz Allen Hamilton, "digital marketing still lags the shift in consumer behavior" prompted by the Internet (Vranica 2007, p. B6). At the same time, the rise of digital communications channels has focused renewed attention on the efficiency and effectiveness of traditional media and the extent to which new media are a complement to or a substitute for television, print, and other established channels—all with an eye toward optimal allocation of marketing mix resources through marketing analytics.

"You have to be able to orchestrate a move toward emerging media," says Greg Welch, head of the CMO practice at Spencer Stuart. "How do you take a traditional media budget and figure out not just how much to allocate to [new] media, but also how to measure it and how to defend it in front of your peer group?" (O'Regan 2007, p. 14). Not surprisingly, many companies have adopted a measured approach to the inclusion of new media in their marketing communication programs until appropriate analytical and modeling techniques can provide better insight into their use. The description of marketing analytics contained in this book offers contemporary perspectives and practices that should provide direction for these marketing mix decisions.

◆ THE MEASURED MARCH TO NEW MEDIA AND MARKETING ANALYTICS

Eighty-plus percent of U.S. consumers are online regularly, and 34% of their media time is spent online. Still, most marketers devote only approximately 5% to 10% of their advertising and promotion dollars to digital media (*Marketing NPV Journal* 2007).

What are the likely reasons for the disconnect between consumer media usage and company media spending? Three are most commonly mentioned: (1) modest budgetary and organizational support for media experimentation, (2) limited business experience with and talent necessary to apply marketing analytics to new media, and

(3) insufficient metrics and marketing analytics to measure the efficiency and effectiveness of new media alongside traditional media.

Slowly Shifting Budget Priorities

Media fragmentation has stretched marketing budgets in many companies. So, too, efforts to create coherent integrated marketing communication campaigns that blend different elements of the traditional communication mix in mutually beneficial ways have placed greater demand on marketing resource allocation and budgeting practices. More often than not, marketers continue to be hamstrung by budgeting policies that do not necessarily support the unique purchase, modeling, measurement, and creative requirements of new media. Moreover, a large portion of the current investment in new media buys and analytics is new money, signifying that senior marketing executives are not yet ready to shift significant portions of their communications budget away from traditional media.

At the same time, communication budgeting policies that explicitly set aside funds for media experimentation are comparatively rare. Industry surveys suggest that approximately one-quarter of large U.S. companies include a designated line item for media experiments in their marketing communications budgets. As for the amount, McKinsey & Company offers a rule of thumb: Spend 75% to 80% of the budget on proven messages that are placed in proven media vehicles and supported by proven dollars. The remaining 20% to 25% of the budget should be allocated to financing well-structured media experiments (Court, Gordon, and Perrey 2005). But there is a hitch. All too often, many companies lack either marketing professionals with substantive new media experience or the specialized talent necessary for conceiving, developing, and delivering digital communications campaigns amenable to meaningful experimentation and measurement. The same can be said of the skills necessary for the application of marketing analytics to marketing mix resource allocation decisions.

New Skills and Structures Are Required but Not Yet Prevalent

Fewer than 24% of senior marketing executives polled by Booz Allen Hamilton in 2007 considered their companies "digitally savvy." A lack of business experience with new media and the dearth of individuals with digital talent were cited as the principal reasons for this situation (Rasmussen, Ude, and Landry 2007). The finding that roughly three in four companies lack the requisite experience and knowledge to engage the digital environment has meant that senior marketing executives must often consider restructuring and repopulating their organizations. According to McKinsey's David Court (2007, p. 29):

> Many of the skills, such as expertise in the business use of social networking, in digital marketing, or in emerging markets, require a degree of specialization that complements the generalist capabilities of traditional marketing managers. As a result, many companies will be forced to restructure their marketing and sales organizations by creating centers of excellence for key marketing capabilities and, perhaps, by outsourcing marketing activities requiring specialized skills, just as some CIOs rely on external IT-development resources. Not surprisingly, almost 75 percent of the chief marketers polled at a recent CMO summit (organized by the Marketing Science Institute and McKinsey) agreed that the skills they needed were becoming so specialized that their organizations would have to operate quite differently in the future.

In a parallel fashion, new technical skills and organizational structures are necessary to bring marketing mix analytics and data-driven econometric models to bear on marketing decisions. Davenport and Harris (2007) emphasize the importance of top-notch analysts familiar with the latest advances in data-collection technology and quantitative analysis. But they forewarn that analysts must express complex ideas and methodology in simple terms and interact productively with marketing decision makers if their talent is to yield better marketing resource allocation decisions. From an organizational perspective, companies such as IBM and Procter & Gamble have created Centers of Excellence to house the marketing analytics capability within their organizations. That said, many marketers still lock in on agreed-on metrics to measure performance and refrain from investing in resources required to build an analytical capability.

Pandora's Box of Metrics and Marketing Analytics

Concern about insufficient metrics and marketing analytics to measure the efficiency and effectiveness of new media has drawn attention to broader questions related to the evaluation of all media performance indicators and the applicability of existing marketing analytics (Bahadur et al. 2007). Call it a virtual Pandora's Box. The number of metrics is not the issue, as new metrics for both traditional and emerging media metrics are being proposed at a breakneck pace (see, e.g., Bucklin, Rutz, and Trusov 2008). Nor is there necessarily a shortage of marketing analytics for different aspects of marketing mix resource allocation and planning (Farris et al. 2006). The true challenge for marketers is determining the quality and appropriateness of these metrics and marketing analytics—in the context of integrated marketing programs—and whether they provide the insights needed to make resource allocation decisions across media.

Without clear metrics that matter and transparent analytical models, senior marketing executives are often at a loss justifying their recommendations to redeploy their marketing mix spending. They need new approaches for linking the marketing spend to financial outcomes—either directly (increased sales) or indirectly (word-of-mouth referrals that lead to customer acquisition). In a 2006 Forrester Research survey, more than 40% of the marketing respondents said that it was too early to tell if they could measure success from their interactive display ads and search marketing programs, even though those were two of the most heavily adopted interactive media (Haven 2007). Not surprisingly, quantifying and measuring the value of marketing programs and investments was identified as the top challenge facing senior marketing executives for 2008, according to a recent poll commissioned by the CMO Council (2008).

◆ PURPOSE OF THE BOOK

Marketing Mix Decisions: New Perspectives and Practices was prepared in response to numerous requests by senior marketing executives and marketing research professionals, at various forums sponsored by the American Marketing Association, to address a pervasive and recurring issue in their companies—namely, marketing mix resource allocation and planning and the application of marketing analytics. This topic has gained momentum as executives have begun to explore and recommend the use of new media as part of their integrated marketing communications programs.

Senior marketing executives and marketing research professionals are the principal audience for this book. The perspectives, practices, and applications described in its content tend to be problem oriented and focus on common issues, questions, and situations faced by marketing practitioners. In this regard, three of the articles provide useful perspectives on the state of knowledge and practice with regard to marketing mix resource allocation and planning. The remaining two articles present evidence-based company case studies that focus on marketing mix resource allocation initiatives and results. When appropriate, the articles offer insights into the possible application of marketing analytics to new media. The five articles contained in the book draw on extensive author experience and knowledge as well as original field-based research.

This book also should be of value to the marketing scholar and educator community. According to Myers, Greyser, and Massey (1979, p. 29), "Understanding practice, and contributing to it, can lead to major contributions to knowledge development." Ideally, the perspectives and practices provided in this book will motivate further scholarly inquiry into the theory and practice of marketing mix resource allocation and planning and will stimulate interest in the inclusion of new media in scholarly research and teaching.

◆ REFERENCES

Bahadur, Nikhil, Patrick W. Houston, Curt Mueller, and Martha Turner (2007), *Not Just Effective but Efficient: A New Blueprint for Marketing in an Era of Fragmented Media*. New York: Booz Allen Hamilton.

Bucklin, Randolph E., Oliver Rutz, and Michael Trusov (2008), "Metrics for the New Internet Marketing Communications Mix," in *Review of Marketing Research*, Vol. 5, Naresh Malhotra, ed. Armonk, NY: M.E. Sharpe.

CMO Council (2008), *Marketing Outlook 2008: Senior Executives Chart a Course for Strategy and Spend*. Palo Alto, CA: CMO Council, (accessed February 9, 2008), [available at http://www.cmocouncil.org/resources].

Court, David (2007), "The Evolving Role of the CMO," *McKinsey Quarterly*, (3), 29.

———, Jonathan Gordon, and Jesko Perrey (2005), "Boosting Returns on Marketing Investment," *McKinsey Quarterly*, (2), 37.

Davenport, Thomas H. and Jeanne G. Harris (2007), *Competing on Analytics: The New Science of Winning*. Boston: Harvard Business School Press.

Farris, Paul W., Neil T. Bendle, Phillip E. Pfeifer, and David J. Reibstein (2006), *Marketing Metrics: 50+ Metrics Every Executive Should Master*. Upper Saddle River, NJ: Wharton School Publishing.

Haven, Brian (2007), "Interactive Marketing Channels to Watch in 2007," Forrester Research, (March 27), (accessed February 9, 2008), [available at http://www.forrester.com/Research/Document/0,7211,41208,00.html].

Kotler, Philip (1971), *Marketing Decision Making: A Model-Building Approach*. New York: Holt, Rinehart and Winston.

Marketing NPV Journal (2007), "A Tipping Point for New Media," 4 (3), 6.

Myers, John, Stephen A. Greyser, and William F. Massey (1979), "The Effectiveness of Marketing's 'R&D' for Marketing Management: An Assessment," *Journal of Marketing*, 43 (January), 17–29.

O'Regan, Rob (2007), "Do You Have What It Takes to Survive as a CMO?" *1to1 Magazine*, (July/August), 14.

Rasmussen, Andrea, Carolyn Ude, and Edward Landry (2007), *HD Marketing 2010: Sharpening the Conversation*. New York: Booz Allen Hamilton.

Vranica, Suzanne (2007), "Password to Marketers' Meeting: Digital," *The Wall Street Journal*, (October 11), B6.

PART ONE

CONTEMPORARY PERSPECTIVES: AN OVERVIEW OF MARKETING MIX RESOURCE ALLOCATION AND PLANNING MODELS AND APPROACHES

The approach companies take for allocating marketing resources ranges from simple heuristics to complex mathematical models. The first selection in this book offers an overview of the more rigorous approaches to marketing mix resource allocation.

In "Allocating Marketing Resources," Harvard Business School researchers Sunil Gupta and Thomas Steenburgh highlight a two-stage approach for marketing resource allocation. In Stage 1, a model of demand is estimated. This model empirically assesses the impact of marketing actions on consumer demand for a company's product. In Stage 2, estimates from the demand model are used as input in an optimization model that attempts to maximize profits. This stage takes into account both costs and a firm's objectives and constraints (e.g., minimum market share requirement).

Over the past several decades, marketing scholars and practitioners have adopted a variety of methods and approaches that explicitly or implicitly follow these two stages. Gupta and Steenburgh categorize these approaches into a 3×3 matrix, which suggests three different approaches for stage-one demand estimation (i.e., decision calculus, experiments, and econometric methods) and three different methods for stage-two economic impact analysis (i.e., descriptive, simulation, and formal optimization approach). Gupta and Steenburgh review the strengths and weaknesses of these approaches and illustrate their use through specific applications and case studies.

CHAPTER 1

ALLOCATING MARKETING RESOURCES

Sunil Gupta, Harvard Business School
Thomas Steenburgh, Harvard Business School

◆ INTRODUCTION

Given that marketing is essential to organic growth, it is not surprising that companies spend billions of dollars on it annually. The total advertising budget of U.S. companies exceeded $285 billion in 2006—more than the gross domestic product of Malaysia, Hong Kong, or New Zealand. Procter & Gamble (P&G) spent more than $4.9 billion in advertising alone in 2006 (*Advertising Age* 2007). Given the magnitude of these expenditures, marketing managers are increasingly being held responsible for their investment decisions and need to demonstrate that their investments generate appropriate returns for the firm.

Allocating marketing resources is a complex series of decisions in a constantly evolving environment. The emergence of new media, such as online search and display advertising, video games, virtual worlds, social networking, online user-generated content, and word-of-mouth marketing (WOM), is creating both new opportunities and new challenges for companies. It is not easy to isolate the effect of a marketing instrument in this dynamic business environment in which multiple factors influence sales and profits. Consequently, many managers continue to rely on simple heuristics and decision rules for resource allocation. For example, a common practice for managers is to use the "percentage-of-sales" rule to allocate their advertising budgets (Lilien, Kotler, and Moorthy 1992). Industry sources commonly publish such advertising-to-sales (A/S) ratios, and managers routinely monitor them. In the sales force arena, Sinha and Zoltner (2001) report that companies typically constrain the ratio of their sales force cost as a percentage of total sales.

An alternative approach is to arrive at the marketing budget from a "bottom-up" method. A manager may determine the advertising budget according to the desired level of brand awareness and the cost of various media vehicles to achieve this awareness. Similarly, in the pharmaceutical industry, a company may decide how many physicians it wants to reach and how frequently they should be contacted. This combination of reach and frequency determines the required size of the sales force (Mantrala 2006). Although such allocation methods are reasonable, in general, they are suboptimal. In examining sales force size and resource allocation studies at 50 companies, Sinha and Zoltner (2001) report that, on average, optimal allocation has the potential to improve a company's contribution by 4.5% over current practices.

The previous approaches all have some merit. They explicitly or implicitly consider a firm's objectives (how many physicians do we wish to reach), its costs (A/S ratio), and its competitive environment (a firm's A/S ratio compared with its competitor's A/S ratio or industry benchmark). However, these methods have limitations. For example, competitive parity (e.g., A/S ratio) is useful only if competitors are equal in strength, have similar objectives, and are acting optimally. Furthermore, these methods are incomplete since they do not account for how markets respond to marketing actions. The purpose of this chapter is to highlight practical approaches that account for costs, customers' responses, and competitors' reactions to marketing actions.

Marketing resource allocation decisions need to be made at several levels—across countries, products, marketing mix elements, and different vehicles within a marketing mix element (e.g., television versus Internet for advertising). Each decision requires some specific considerations. For example, when allocating resources across countries, managers need to account for both country-specific factors (e.g., growth, local environment) and spillover effects of marketing actions across countries. Similarly, the allocation of resources across products requires careful consideration of the substitution and complementary nature of the products (Duvvuri, Ansari, and Gupta 2007; Manchanda, Ansari, and Gupta 1999). Despite these differences, many fundamental elements are common across all these decisions—for example, how do customers respond to changes in a marketing action. In this chapter, we focus on these common themes. The majority of our discussion centers on marketing resource allocation for a single product, though the basic approaches can be extended to other scenarios.

Finally, this chapter addresses rigorous but practical approaches to marketing resource allocation. As such, we draw on academic research and practical examples that address real-world situations rather than small-scale lab studies or theoretical models. Although the latter play a strong role in developing theories as well as improving our understanding of a certain phenomenon, we are primarily interested in how these theories can be applied in practice. Given this focus, we do not intend this chapter to be a literature review of academic work, nor a roadmap for future research. Our purpose is simply to develop a framework that is useful for managers who are responsible for allocating marketing resources for their products and services.

◆ APPROACHES FOR RESOURCE ALLOCATION

The process of marketing resource allocation consists of two stages. In Stage 1, a model of demand is estimated. This model empirically assesses the impact of marketing actions on consumer demand of a company's product. Ideally, the model also includes competitive activities. While in some cases data on competitors' actions are available (e.g., scanner data studies for consumer packaged goods), in many other scenarios, these data are not known (e.g., in database marketing).

In Stage 2, estimates from the demand model are used as input in an optimization model that attempts to assess the economic impact of marketing actions. This stage takes into account both costs and a company's objectives and constraints (e.g., minimum market share requirement). Although most optimization models do not account for competitive reactions to changes in a target firm's marketing budget, more sophisticated models can consider these reactions through either simulation or game-theoretic equilibrium models.

Over the past several decades, marketing researchers and practitioners have adopted various methods and approaches that explicitly or implicitly follow these two stages. In Table 1.1, we categorize these approaches into a 3 × 3 matrix, which suggests three different

Table 1.1 ♦ Demand Estimation and Economic Impact Analysis

		Demand Estimation		
		Decision Calculus	Experiments	Econometric
Economic Impact Analysis	Descriptive		Godes and Mayzlin (2007) Anderson and Simester (2004)	Wittink (2002)
	What-if			Jedidi, Mela, and Gupta (1999)
	Optimization	Lodish (1971)		Steenburgh, Ainslie, and Engebretson (2003) Tirenni et al. (2007)

approaches for Stage 1 demand estimation and three different methods for Stage 2 economic impact analysis. We begin by describing the pros and cons of each option at a high level in the remainder of this section. We go into greater depth in the next section by discussing specific examples of how researchers have used the techniques to address issues commonly encountered in practice.

Demand Estimation (Stage 1)

There are three broad approaches for demand estimation, as Table 1.1 shows. Each approach has advantages and disadvantages, and each is more suitable in some situations than others.

Decision Calculus

In his classic article, Little (1970, p. B466) laments that "the big problem with management science models is that managers practically never use them." He argues that models should be simple, robust, easy to control by managers, adaptive to changing environments, complete on important issues, and easy to communicate. However, most models fail to meet these requirements. It is difficult to find good models that are simple and yet include all the information relevant for a complex business environment. It is even more difficult to obtain appropriate data to empirically estimate these models. This prompted Little to coin the term "decision calculus" to describe models in which managerial judgment is used as input.

In many situations, the decision calculus approach is perhaps the only way to build a demand model. Consider a firm that wants to decide on the optimal number of times its sales force should call on physicians. If this company always used a certain call frequency in the past, it has no practical way of determining how changes in the call pattern might affect demand. A lack of historical variation in call patterns and practical difficulties in conducting experiments leave the firm few options on which to build such a model. Decision calculus uses managerial input to estimate the demand function that can be subsequently used in Stage 2 for optimization (Lodish 1971).

Since Little's (1970) article, a series of studies have used decision calculus to calibrate demand models and allocate resources successfully (some recent examples include Divakar, Ratchford, and Shankar 2005; Natter et al. 2007; Wierenga, Van Bruggen, and Staelin 1999). In two forecasting situations in which managers made real-time forecasts, Blattberg and Hoch (1986) show that statistical models and managerial judgment achieved about the same level of predictive accuracy, while a combination of model and manager outperformed either decision input alone. They suggest that though models are better at combining complex data in a consistent an unbiased fashion, managers are better at incorporating intangible insights about the market and the competitive environment.

In general, decision calculus provides a useful approach for demand estimation using managerial judgment when a company does not have historical data and cannot afford to do experiments, whether because of a lack of money or time. This approach is also appropriate if there are dramatic changes in the industry, a firm's environment, or its strategy. For example, managers face uncertainty and challenges in allocating resources to new media, such as keyword searches, social networks, or buzz marketing. However, these managers have significant experience in traditional advertising and its effectiveness. Their experience and expertise in advertising can provide them a strong benchmark for the potential effectiveness of new media channels (e.g., knowing that the traditional advertising elasticity is .1, a manager can judge whether new media are likely to be twice as effective). These starting benchmarks can be updated as managers gain more experience with the new media channels.

A decision calculus approach might also be appropriate if managers are willing to use a model that considers their personal knowledge and expertise. A key strength (and, at the same time, a key limitation) of this approach is its reliance on managerial input, which can be biased. We refer the interested reader to Eisenstein and Lodish (2002), who review the marketing literature on this approach and provide guidance to researchers and practitioners on how to improve them.

Experiments

Experiments provide a useful way to assess consumers' responses to stimuli. By allowing a manager to control for factors that otherwise might influence the outcome, experiments enable him or her to isolate the impact of the marketing instrument under study. Experiments are also useful in gauging consumer response to new activities that the firm has not tried historically.

Catalog and credit card companies with millions of customers find it very useful to set up test-and-control samples to assess the effectiveness of various direct marketing programs. Consumer packaged goods companies have frequently conducted advertising experiments in matching cities. The advent of technology has now made it possible to conduct split-cable television experiments with test-and-control households in the same city to assess the effectiveness of various advertising creatives and budgets (Lodish et al. 1995). Experiments such as conjoint analysis are routinely used for new product design and to find consumers' price sensitivity. Harrah's Entertainment has used experiments very effectively to offer the right reward to the right customers at the right time (Loveman 2003).

In general, experiments provide a useful way to gauge consumers' responses to a marketing action when a firm can afford to subject test-and-control samples to different treatments. In some situations, however, this is not feasible. For example, if a firm wishes to test a new compensation system or organization structure for its sales force, it may not be practically possible to have two different systems or structures for the test-and-control groups. In general, experiments are good at obtaining the short-term impact of an action. Although it is possible to find the long-term effects of marketing actions through experiments, it becomes practically difficult to control environmental and competitive changes for a very long period. Finally, experiments can become very complex with an increasing number of factors to test. This requires a manager to carefully consider only a few critical factors that need to be tested.

These critical factors can be determined in three ways. First, the choice of factors is governed by the decision objectives of a manager. For example, a manager in charge of allocating resources for a catalog company needs to know to whom to send catalogs and how often, since catalogs form a large part of the budget. Second, prior experience and knowledge of the business gives a manager a good sense of the key business drivers. A knowledgeable manager should know whether pricing, advertising, or distribution is critical for the growth of the business. Third, similar in spirit to the multiphase trials in the pharmaceutical industry, managers can conduct small-scale experiments to determine which factors have the most impact on sales and profit. These subsets of factors can then be tested in greater detail in a large-scale experiment.

Econometric Approaches

With the increasing availability of data, improved computer power, and advances in econometrics, companies can now easily harness their historical data to estimate the impact of various marketing instruments on consumer demand. In the consumer packaged goods industry, the advent of scanner data has revolutionized marketing resource allocation through this approach.[1] A large number of academic studies have built models to understand the effectiveness of sales promotions and advertising (Guadagni and Little 1983; Gupta 1988; Tellis 1988). Many studies have also teased out the short- and long-term impact of these actions (Jedidi, Mela, and Gupta 1999; Mela, Gupta, and Lehmann 1997; Pauwels, Siddarth, and Hanssens 2002). Companies such as Information Resources Inc. and Nielsen routinely offer marketing mix models based on these data as a service to their clients. Client firms, such as Campbell, actively monitor their marketing resource allocation according to the results of these models.

Econometric studies have also found significant use in database marketing. A large number of studies have used companies' historical data on RFM (recency, frequency, and monetary value) to build models that estimate consumer response to marketing campaigns. These models significantly improve marketing resource allocation by providing powerful insights about who should be contacted, when, and how frequently (Gupta et al. 2006; Venkatesan and Kumar 2004).

Econometric approaches use a firm's historical data and allow a manager to build models that capture the complexity of the business. These methods provide accurate and unbiased assessments of marketing effectiveness. They enable a firm to constantly learn and adapt from its previous efforts. The models are also transportable across products and geographies and thus provide a common language across the organization. When a company has limited historical data (e.g., for a new product introduction), it can still employ this approach by using analogies or meta-analysis priors, which can be updated in a Bayesian fashion using current data on the new product.

An econometric approach is most useful when markets are relatively stable such that historical estimates provide a good indicator of the future market conditions. A method based on historical data is unable to capture situations in which the industry dynamics or a firm's strategy has undergone major changes. Therefore, model recommendations are relevant only within the range of historical data.

Economic Impact Analysis (Stage 2)

Stage 1 provides estimates of how marketing actions influence market demand. These estimates become the input for Stage 2, in which a firm decides on optimal resource allocation that maximizes its profits. As indicated in Table 1.1, there are three broad approaches in Stage 2.

Descriptive Approach

A descriptive approach uses parameter estimates of the demand equation to make directional recommendations. For example, high consumer price sensitivity for a brand might suggest the allocation of more promotional dollars to this brand. Parameter estimates can be converted into demand elasticities, which can be compared across various marketing instruments to guide resource allocation (Steenburgh 2007). For example, in a large-scale study for the pharmaceutical industry, Wittink (2002) found very low elasticity for direct-to-consumer (DTC) advertising. He further converted these elasticities into return on investment (ROI) to show that investment in DTC advertising does not pay off. At minimum, his results provide directional guidance to pharmaceutical managers to cut down on their DTC budgets.

A descriptive approach is simple and easy to use. It is the natural outcome of demand analysis in Stage 1 and requires little additional analytical work. However, as models become complex with interactions among marketing elements, the descriptive approach is less suitable to isolate the effects of each marketing action. For example, it may be straightforward to see the short-term effect of advertising on sales using this method. However, it is more difficult to use this approach to assess the net effect of advertising on sales that takes into account not only the short-term effects but also the long-term impact on brand health and consumers' price sensitivity. This approach also does not take competitive reactions into account, so it is better suited to understanding how the world works today rather than how it will work if major changes are undertaken.

Simulation or "What-if" Analysis

To handle such complex interactions, optimal resource allocation can be achieved using simulations or "what-if" analyses. Effectively, a manager can try various marketing plans as inputs into the demand model and simulate the effects on sales and profits. Increasing computer power makes it easy to conduct hundreds of such simulations in a short period. The model complexities are preserved, and the user does not need to make subjective interpretations about the interactions between various marketing elements. A wide array of simulations can also build confidence in the robustness of the results. For example, if profits do not change significantly with large changes in advertising, a manager can safely conclude that other elements of the marketing mix deserve more attention.

Simulations have two key limitations. First, as the number of options (marketing actions and their budget levels) increases, the potential combinations for simulation can increase exponentially. Second, simulation is effectively a coarse grid search over the profit function. In other words, it provides an approximation rather than an exact solution to the optimization problem.

Optimization

The most sophisticated and complex approach is to build a formal optimization model that uses demand parameters from Stage 1 as inputs and sets up a profit function that is maximized using operations research algorithms. These algorithms may include linear, integer, or dynamic programming methods. This approach also allows managers to put in business constraints as part of the optimization algorithm. For example, from his or her understanding of the business and the market, a manager may decide that it is absolutely essential to have a certain minimum level of advertising.

In general, optimization methods take two approaches for estimation. An "elegant" approach is to find a closed-form mathematical solution to the optimization problem. However, a more practical approach is to conduct a numerical grid search over the parameter space to find optimal or near-optimal solutions.

On the positive side, this approach provides a comprehensive solution to the resource allocation problem by searching over the entire space of options. At the same time, as the complexity of the problem and the number of options increase, it is more difficult to use this approach. Consequently, many studies simplify the problem by dealing with only one or two marketing elements at a time.

♦ APPLICATIONS

In this section, we discuss a few applications of the previously discussed methodologies. Our goal is to provide concrete examples of each methodology to promote understanding of how it can be used rather than to provide an exhaustive list of research on each topic. For each application, we briefly describe the managerial problem, the research approach used to solve the problem, and the results obtained from this approach.

Experiments (Stage 1) and Descriptive Analysis (Stage 2)

We describe two studies that used experiments. The first study examined the effectiveness of WOM communication, and the second study allocated promotional dollars between new and existing customers of a catalog company.

Effectiveness of WOM Communication

Problem. The impact of "new media" on marketing and advertising is continually being revised upward. Online search and display advertising, video games, virtual worlds, social networking, online user-generated content, and WOM marketing are growing by leaps and bounds as companies address the fragmentation of consumer markets and the swing from mass to niche marketing. According to a recent survey by McKinsey & Company, one-third of the companies that advertise online are already spending more than 10% of their advertising budgets there (Bughin, Erbenich, and Shenkan 2007).

Traditional marketing giants such as Unilever and P&G are embracing new media. Unilever has gained significant attention with its campaigns for Dove and Axe, the success of which was driven virally by Web sites, blogs, and YouTube. Since 2001, P&G has been building Tremor, a WOM network services company, which includes two consumer panels: Vocalpoint, which consists of 450,000 mothers of children under 19 years of age,[2] and Tremor Teen, a network of 230,000 teenagers aged 13–19.[3] Procter & Gamble claims that the members (or "connectors" as the company refers to them) are a select group of consumers who talk to their friends more than the average person. For example, P&G boasts that Vocalpoint mothers talk to 20–25 people every day, compared with the average mother who only talks to 5 people a day.

Godes and Mayzlin (2007) report several other examples in which companies promoted their products and services through WOM marketing. For example, in 2001, Hasbro promoted its new handheld video game *POX* through 1600 "cool" kids of Chicago elementary schools. In September 2005, NBC promoted its reality show about weight loss, *The Biggest Loser,* by encouraging its 1000 biggest fans to throw parties during an advanced screening of the show's premiere. In 2006, WD-40 used P&G's Vocalpoint to promote its new product extension, the "No-Mess" pen.

Despite companies' foray into new media and buzz marketing, several questions remain. How effective is WOM in generating sales? Can firms create WOM, or is it a naturally occurring phenomenon that is not under an advertiser's control? Who are better disseminators of WOM?

Approach. Godes and Mayzlin (2007) address these questions through a field experiment conducted by BzzAgent, an agency for Rock Bottom Brewery, a restaurant chain. At the time of the study, Rock Bottom Brewery did business in 15 markets across the United States, with annual gross sales of approximately $100 million. The company maintained a loyalty program with several thousand customers as members.

For the field test, Godes and Mayzlin recruited 381 of the firm's loyal customers. In addition, they recruited 692 "agents" of BzzAgent. This agency maintains a panel of agents who are encouraged to create WOM for a client's products or services. The purpose of recruiting loyal customers of the firm and noncustomers (agents of BzzAgent) was to compare the WOM effectiveness of the two groups. The WOM creation process ran for a product category in 15 markets for approximately 13 weeks (April to June 2003). Participants were asked to report their WOM creation activity by filling in a report on a Web site each time they engaged in a WOM episode. BzzAgent then graded each report on its potential to create meaningful WOM. (Participants were given an incentive to create meaningful WOM since higher scores entitled them to win prizes. The average prize was valued at $15.) Godes and Mayzlin also obtained weekly sales data for each of the 15 markets for the campaign period as well as for the same period from the previous year. There was natural variation in the WOM creation across the 15 markets. To assess the impact of WOM on sales, Godes and Mayzlin ran a fixed-effects regression model, which controlled for week and market effects.

Results. Godes and Mayzlin (2007) found that not all WOM is created equal. Specifically, the impact of WOM created by customers with no relationship with the firm had a much greater impact on sales than the WOM created by the company's loyal customers. This seemingly counterintuitive result is actually consistent with the theory of weak ties (Granovetter 1973), which suggests that WOM through acquaintances has significantly more impact than WOM through those with stronger ties in a social network. In a way, this suggests that customers unconnected to the firm are likely to be less biased and more believable and therefore should be weighed more heavily in terms of their impact on WOM. Godes and Mayzlin also found that each WOM referral from noncustomers yielded average incremental sales of $192. These results provide useful guidelines on how much resources the company should spend on WOM marketing campaigns.

Kumar, Petersen, and Leone (2007) use a survey method to assess the value of WOM and referral. They polled 9900 customers of a telecommunications firm and 6700 customers of a financial services firm on their referral intention. Then, they tracked these customers' behavior and the behavior of the prospective customers who the referring customers brought in over time. They also adjusted for the possibility that some of the prospecting customers would have joined the service anyway. Several interesting results emerged from their study. First, less than half the customers who indicated their intention to refer their friend to the company's services actually did so (for the financial services firm, 68% intended to refer friends but only 33% did so; for the telecommunications firm, of 81% intenders, only 30% followed through). Second, very few of the referrals actually generated customers (14% at the financial services firm and 12% at the telecommunications firm). Furthermore, of the prospects who did become customers, very few were profitable (11% for the financial services firm and 8% for the telecommunications firm).

Allocating Promotional Dollars

Problem. Anderson and Simester (2004) describe a situation in which a catalog company wanted to understand how to allocate promotional dollars between new and established customers. The firm was also concerned that promotion might have a negative long-term impact on consumers' repeat purchase behavior. The company, a medium-sized retailer, sold approximately 450 products targeted at well-educated older customers. In general, the products were experience goods, similar to books and software. Historically, the company had offered a variety of discounts ranging from under 20% off the regular price to as much as 70%. The majority of its sales were promotions ranging between 20% and 60% discounts, with 20%–30% discounts accounting for almost one-third of overall sales.

Approach. To understand the long-term effects of promotion depth on new and established customers, Anderson and Simester (2004) conducted three large-scale field experiments. Study A was conducted with established customers of the firm. A control version of the catalog was sent to 37,758 randomly selected customers. This catalog presented 86 products on 72 pages. The average promotional discount in the control condition was 30% off the regular price. A randomly selected set of 18,708 customers received a promotional or test catalog in which 36 of the 86 products were offered at an average discount of 60% (instead of 30% for the control condition). The price on the remaining 50 products remained the same in both the test and the control conditions.

Results. From the control group, 761 customers, or 2.02%, bought from the catalog, while the promotional catalog generated a response from 597, or 3.19%, of the customers. Customers from the test group ordered an average of 2.14 units at an average price of $78.51, while control group customers ordered an average of 1.59 units at an average price of $124.03. These customers were then tracked for the next 28 months, and both groups received the same catalogs. Future purchase behavior revealed that compared with the control group, customers from the test group purchased fewer products (6.89 versus 7.67) and less expensive items (average price $84.86 versus $95.51). As a result, the overall future revenue per customer was sharply lower among customers in the test condition ($584.68 versus $733.50). In other words, increasing the depth of promotion had a negative long-term effect among established customers (see Table 1.2).

Anderson and Simester (2004) conducted two additional studies with new or prospective customers. These studies were similar to Study A, and we provide their details in Table 1.2. In contrast to the results of Study A with established customers, Studies B and C with new customers showed *exactly the opposite results.* Specifically, although increasing the depth of discounts had a negative long-term effect among established customers (Study A), it had a significant, positive long-term effect among new customers. Although these results do not provide an optimal promotional discount value, they provide good direction to the company on how to allocate its promotional dollars among new and established customers.

It is common practice among catalog companies to conduct such experiments. In 1999, more than 31% of catalog firms reported conducting split-sample experiments of pricing strategies (Direct Marketing Association 2000). Experiments are also commonly employed for the testing of advertising budgets and creative. For

Table 1.2 ♦ Long-Term Effects of Promotion Depth on New and Established Customers

Customers	Study A Established	Study B New	Study C New
Sample Size			
Test	18,708	148,702	146,774
Control	35,758	148,703	97,847
Average % Discount in Promotion Version	42	47	42
Number of pages in catalog	72	8	16
Number of products	86	16	36
Number of prices varied	36	14	32
Number of months of future data	28	24	22
Purchases from the Test Catalog[a]			
% who purchased	158	185	174
Units ordered per customer	135	116	130
Average unit price ($)	63	65	71
Repeat Purchases from Future Catalogs[a]			
Units ordered per customer	90	114	136
Average unit price ($)	89	96	90

[a]These measures are all indexed to 100 in the respective control condition.

Adapted from Anderson, Eric and Duncan Simester (2004), "Long Run Effects of Promotion Depth on New Versus Established Customers: Three Field Studies," *Marketing Science*, 23 (1), 4–20. Reprinted with permission from the Institute for Operations Research and Management Sciences.

example, Eastlack and Rao (1986) report an advertising experiment for V8 vegetable juice. In this experiment, they varied the advertising budget, creative, and the media mix between radio and television across various markets to examine the effect of these elements. Using this experimental data, they also estimated the S-shaped advertising response function to determine both the threshold or minimum level of advertising and the saturation or maximum level of advertising.

Lodish and colleagues (1995) examined 389 real-world split-cable television advertising experiments[4] and found that the average advertising elasticity for new products was much higher (.26) than that for established products (.05). They also found that television advertising was more likely to work when there were accompanying changes in ad creative and media strategy.

Econometric Estimation (Stage 1) and Descriptive Analysis (Stage 2)

Problem. Allocating the budget across marketing instruments is challenging for every organization. For example, for pharmaceutical firms, the key issue is how to allocate resources among elements such as detailing to physicians, journal advertising, physician meetings, and DTC advertising.

Turf battles can make the allocation process as much about building the biggest fiefdom as about making the right decisions for the company. The sales organization is bound to ask whether marketing really needs to create more ads, and marketing is bound to ask whether more salespeople are really needed in the field. When a history of data exists, estimating the historical ROI for each marketing instrument is one way to take the emotion out of the budgeting process and help the firm allocate its marketing dollars more effectively.

Approach. In a broad study of the pharmaceutical drug market, Wittink (2002) assessed the ROI of several marketing instruments during the 1995–2000 period. His study was based on drugs that produced at least $25 million in revenue in 2000, which resulted in 392 branded and 127 generic drugs being included. In Stage 1 demand estimation, Wittink used standard regression analysis to determine the relationship between unit sales and each of the marketing instruments. Instruments used to market pharmaceutical drugs include detailing, physician meetings, journal advertising, and DTC advertising. The first three elements are directed only at physicians, while DTC advertising may be seen by physicians but is primarily directed at consumers.

The effectiveness of the marketing instruments was believed to depend on the drugs' size and the length of time they had been on the market. To control for these factors, each drug was classified into one of nine categories according to its sales revenue and launch year. The revenue categories were $25–$100 million, $101–$500 million, and greater than $500 million, and the launch year categories were pre-1994, 1994–1997, and 1998–2000. Table 1.3 characterizes how the marketing expenditures varied across the various categories of drugs. The first value in a cell is the percentage of products that had expenditures in at least one month during the study period for a given marketing instrument, and the second value is the average monthly expenditure. To illustrate, 94% of the drugs that produced $25–$100 million in revenue and that were launched before 1994 devoted at least some money to detailing. For the brands with at least some detailing, the average monthly expenditure was $155 million.

Detailing was the best-used marketing instrument, being employed by more than 90% of the drugs across all classifications, and it always had the highest average spending. The other physician-directed marketing instruments—physician meetings and journal

Table 1.3 ◆ Descriptive Statistics of the Pharmaceutical Data

A: Brands with More Than $500 Million in Revenue

	Launch Year		
	<1994	1994–1997	1998–2000
DET	100%[a] / $2,758[b]	100% / $3,206	100% / $6,607
PME	100% / $427	100% / $698	100% / $1,917
JAD	92% / $129	100% / $245	100% / $532
DTC	67% / $605	67% / $1,224	78% / $2,482

B: Brands with $101–$500 Million in Revenue

	<1994	1994–1997	1998–2000
DET	100% / $732	100% / $1,098	95% / $1,711
PME	93% / $73	95% / $210	95% / $439
JAD	79% / $41	98% / $113	100% / $161
DTC	26% / $38	53% / $272	38% / $949

C: Brands with $25–$100 Million in Revenue

	<1994	1994–1997	1998–2000
DET	94% / $155	92% / $460	100% / $1,144
PME	85% / $13	89% / $56	86% / $180
JAD	73% / $8	92% / $36	100% / $148
DTC	10% / $13	24% / $45	21% / $5

[a]Percentage of products with expenditures on this marketing instrument in at least one month during the study period.

[b]Average monthly expenditure in millions of dollars.

Notes: DET = physician detailing, PME = physician meetings, and JAD = journal advertising.

Source: Wittink, Dick R. (2002), "Analysis of ROI for Pharmaceutical Promotion (ARPP)," white paper presentation to the Association of Medical Publications, (September 18), (accessed February 21, 2008), [available at http://www.vioworks.com/clients/amp].

advertising—were also widely used, being employed by at least 73% of the drugs across all classifications and often by more than 90% of the drugs. Direct-to-consumer advertising was the least-used marketing instrument, implemented by between 10% and 78% of the drugs across the different classifications. However, the average monthly expenditures devoted to this instrument were sometimes quite high.

Results. We now turn our attention to marketing ROI. These calculations are interpreted as the estimated increase in revenue for a $1 increase in spending on a marketing instrument. Therefore, an ROI with a value less than $1 suggests that the incremental marketing spending would not pay for itself through increased sales. These numbers should not be interpreted as one marketing instrument being more effective than another, per se, as the ROI values are also influenced by the amount of money being spent on the instrument.

The ROI for brands with revenues greater than $500 million is listed in Table 1.4, Panel A. The values of the physician-directed instruments (detailing, physician meetings, and journal advertising) are fairly consistent and are all greater than $1. Furthermore, the marketing spending is more effective for newer drugs than for older ones. A marketing dollar spent on a drug launched before 1994 returns approximately $3 in revenue, while a dollar spent on a drug launched between 1998 and 2000 returns approximately $12 in revenue. In comparison, the ROI on DTC advertising is much lower. Spending on DTC advertising pays for itself only when it is used on recently launched drugs, and even in this case, it is a relatively small ROI of $1.3.

A similar pattern of ROI arises for the 192 drugs that produce revenues between $100 and $500 million. The effectiveness of the marketing spending is greater for the physician-directed marketing

Table 1.4 ♦ Return on Investment for Pharmaceutical Marketing

A: Brands with more than $500 Million in Revenue

	Launch Year		
	<1994	1994–1997	1998–2000
DET	$3.1[a]	$5.9	$11.6
PME	$3.1	$6.0	$11.7
JAD	$3.1	$6.2	$12.2
DTC	$.4	$.7	$1.3

B: Brands with $100–$500 Million in Revenue

	<1994	1994–1997	1998–2000
DET	$1.2	$1.6	$2.1
PME	$2.0	$2.7	$3.6
JAD	$2.3	$3.1	$4.2
DTC	$.1	$.2	$.2

C: Brands with $25–$100 Million in Revenue

	<1994	1994–1997	1998–2000
DET	$.9	$1.0	$1.0
PME	$.1	$.1	$.1
JAD	$6.2	$6.7	$7.2
DTC	$.0	$.0	$.0

[a]For example, a $1 increase in DET would generate an incremental revenue of $3.1.

Notes: DET = physician detailing, PME = physician meetings, and JAD = journal advertising.

Source: Wittink, Dick R. (2002), "Analysis of ROI for Pharmaceutical Promotion (ARPP)," white paper presentation to the Association of Medical Publications, (September 18), (accessed February 21, 2008), [available at http://www.vioworks.com/clients/amp].

instruments than for DTC advertising, and the effectiveness is greater for more recently launched drugs than for older drugs (see Table 1.4, Panel B). Nevertheless, the overall ROI is smaller for intermediate-revenue drugs. For the physician-directed instruments, the ROI ranges between $1.2 and $2.3 for the oldest drugs (compared with $3 for the largest drugs) and between $2.1 and $4.6 for the newest drugs (compared with $12 for the largest drugs). Furthermore, DTC advertising never pays for itself for the intermediate drugs, as the ROI increases for more recent launch dates but still ranges between $.1 and $.2.

For the 137 brands that produce the lowest revenues, we observe a different pattern of results (see Table 1.4, Panel C). Not all physician-directed spending yields positive ROI, as physician meetings are $.1 regardless of the launch date and detailing ranges between $.9 and $1.0. Journal advertising is the only instrument that pays for itself, with an ROI ranging between $6.2 and $7.2. Furthermore, while the ROI increases for more recently launched drugs, it does not change much across launch dates. All else being equal, firms might consider directing more money toward journal advertising and less money toward detailing and physician meetings for these drugs. Similar to the intermediate- and large-revenue drugs, DTC advertising does not pay for itself, as it yields an ROI of zero.

Although the ROI numbers do not tell us what the optimal spending levels are for each marketing instrument, they do give us a better sense of how companies might reallocate their marketing dollars. We would expect firms to shift their spending away from instruments that produce low ROI and toward investments that produce high ROI, keeping other organizational goals in mind. For example, a company might continue to invest in detailing, even if the ROI is not justified, if it has strategic interest in maintaining a sales force to sell upcoming products. Calculating the ROI, however, can help the firm make better trade-offs when making these types of decisions.

Econometric Estimation (Stage 1) and What-if Analysis (Stage 2)

Problem. Allocating resources between advertising and trade or consumer promotions is a topic of constant debate and discussion in most organizations. Proponents of advertising claim that advertising builds brand equity and insulates a brand from price changes in the marketplace. Supporters of promotions highlight dramatic market response to short-term promotions as evidence of their effectiveness. However, it is much easier to assess the short-term effects of promotions (e.g., Guadagni and Little 1983; Gupta 1988) than it is to determine the long-term effects of promotions and advertising. Do promotions have a negative long-term impact on a brand? Do these negative long-term effects outweigh the positive short-term effects of promotions? If we take into account both the short- and long-term effects, what is the optimal allocation of resources between advertising and promotions? Jedidi, Mela, and Gupta (1999) address these questions for a consumer packaged goods product.

Approach. Jedidi, Mela, and Gupta (1999) used eight years of disaggregate data (1984–1992) on four brands in a consumer nonfood category for 691 households. Descriptive statistics of the data are given in Table 1.5. Jedidi, Mela, and Gupta used discrete choice models to capture consumers' decisions of which brand to buy and how much quantity to buy as a function of consumer characteristics and marketing activity (regular price, temporary price reduction due to promotion and advertising). They further postulated that promotion and advertising can have long-term effects on consumer purchases in two ways: by influencing the brand equity and by affecting consumers' price sensitivity. They estimated the demand model (Stage 1) using a maximum-likelihood procedure. In the second stage, they conducted simulations to assess the managerial implications of these results for resource allocation. These simulations also included competitive reaction functions. Jedidi, Mela, and Gupta argued that simulating the effect of a change in marketing activity of a brand—for example, an increase in discounts—in the absence of competitive reaction could lead to an optimistic assessment of these effects.

Results. The results of this study showed that, as expected, promotions had a positive and significant impact on consumer choice in the short run. In the long run, advertising improved brand equity, while promotions had a negative impact on brand equity. Furthermore, frequent promotions made consumers less promotion sensitive in their brand choice and more promotion sensitive in their quantity decision. In other words, frequent promotion of brands made it unnecessary for consumers to switch brands and made them more likely to stockpile when their favorite brand was on promotion.

These results are intuitively appealing, but they do not provide any specific directions for resource allocation. That is, they still do not tell us whether the positive short-term effects of promotions are outweighed by promotions' negative long-term effects. To address this question, Jedidi, Mela, and Gupta conducted simulations. These analyses first estimated baseline sales and profits in the absence of

Table 1.5 ♦ Descriptive Statistics of Jedidi, Mela, and Gupta's (1999) Data

Variable	Brand	Mean for 1984–1987	Mean for 1988–1991
Market share	1	.35	.36
	2	.11	.13
	3	.16	.13
	4	.10	.12
Purchase quantity per occasion (oz.)	1	27.72	28.41
	2	26.20	28.58
	3	28.04	30.27
	4	28.60	29.42
Regular price per ounce ($)	1	.051	.054
	2	.050	.055
	3	.052	.056
	4	.048	.053
Promotion frequency (% of occasions)	1	15.4	33.4
	2	8.7	32.6
	3	10.2	25.3
	4	6.4	29.8
Promotion depth (% off)	1	11.3	17.9
	2	12.1	17.3
	3	13.8	16.8
	4	29.8	20.2
Advertising[a]	1	66.61	29.78
	2	25.52	17.55
	3	45.26	26.70
	4	28.98	12.25

[a]Advertising represents average inflation-adjusted advertising dollars in thousands spent in a quarter.

Source: Jedidi, Kamel, Carl F. Mela, and Sunil Gupta (1999), "Managing Advertising and Promotion for Long-Run Profitability," *Marketing Science*, 18 (1), 1–22. Reprinted with permission from the Institute for Operations Research and Management Sciences.

any changes in marketing policy. Then, price, promotion, or advertising of a target brand was changed by 5%, and its impact on both competitive and consumer responses was simulated on the basis of the Stage 1 models. The results of this simulation are presented in Table 1.6.

The results showed that increasing promotion depth or frequency decreased profits of all four brands. However, increasing advertising had mixed effects on brand profitability. It marginally improved the profits of only one brand, while profits for three other brands went down.

Table 1.6 ♦ Long-Term Impact of Changes in Promotion and Advertising on Profits

% Change in Profit with 5% Increase in	Brand 1	Brand 2	Brand 3	Brand 4
Advertising	−.02	.13	−.69*	−.32*
Promotion frequency	−.33*	−.33*	−.33*	−.31*
Promotion depth	−.38*	−.49*	−.31*	−.31*

*Significant at the .05 level.

Adapted from Jedidi, Kamel, Carl F. Mela, and Sunil Gupta (1999), "Managing Advertising and Promotion for Long-Run Profitability," *Marketing Science*, 18 (1), 1–22. Reprinted with permission from the Institute for Operations Research and Management Sciences.

Two broader conclusions emerge from this study. First, it is perhaps too simplistic to suggest that firms should increase advertising or cut promotions. This decision needs to be made on a case-by-case basis depending on each brand's current advertising and promotion budget as well as its position in the marketplace. Second, it is remarkable to see that a 5% increase in advertising or promotions has less than a 1% effect on profits. This seems to suggest that the market is operating efficiently and that managers in this product category are making decisions that are close to optimal.

Many studies employ this approach of estimating a demand model using the econometric method in Stage 1 and then conducting simulations to derive optimal resource allocation in Stage 2. Duvvuri, Ansari, and Gupta (2007) built a model for retailers in which they account for cross-category complementarities. Using data from six product categories, they showed that discounts in one category (e.g., spaghetti) can affect the purchase in the target category as well as its complementary category (e.g., sauce). Their simulations further showed that the average profitability gain from targeted customer discounts over nontargeted discounts is only 1.29% if these complementarities are ignored. However, profit gain is almost 8.26% when these complementarities are included.

Decision Calculus (Stage 1) and Optimization (Stage 2)

Problem. Although all salespeople face the problem of how to allocate effort across customers, there is little consistency in how they address the issue. Some salespeople essentially ignore the problem by spending most of their time with the customers who like them the best.

Others simply base their current calling schedules on historical visitation patterns or develop rules of thumb to help manage the allocation task, for example, by making one call per month for every $100,000 that an account bills. These heuristics may be systematic, but they do not necessarily meet the overall goals of the firm. If there are diminishing returns to the number of visits, a salesperson may be better off spending less time with his or her biggest accounts and more time with prospects and smaller accounts.

In lieu of these heuristics, the firm would like the salesperson to choose a calling pattern that maximizes some objective (e.g., profit, but many others are possible), but several issues stand in the way. First, it is often difficult to build a statistical model with historical data that adequately predicts how an individual salesperson will fare with an individual customer. Personal selling is a unique endeavor, so one salesperson may thrive in a given account while another may struggle. Furthermore, although much progress has been made over the years, statistical models can have some difficulty in capturing account-by-account nuances, and data limitations may require models to be developed on a more aggregate basis. Furthermore, salespeople tend to favor their own judgment over statistical models. Thus, they are more likely to follow a recommendation if it takes their knowledge and experience into account and if they understand why it is being made.

Approach. Lodish (1971) developed an interactive computer system, named CALLPLAN, to address this problem. CALLPLAN divided the salesperson's underlying time allocation problem into two stages. In the first stage, the expected contribution of all possible calling policies was independently determined for every prospect and account using the decision calculus approach. In the second stage, a mathematical program was used to determine the best possible calling schedule. CALLPLAN maximized the salesperson's total contribution across all accounts by considering the returns from all possible calling schedules in light of the limited amount of time a salesperson could work. The number of possible calling schedules an individual salesperson would be able to calculate without the aid of a computer is limited, but CALLPLAN was able to process this information very efficiently.

CALLPLAN was designed to be used by a salesperson in conjunction with his or her manager. This required the system to be easy to use and understand and the outputs to be quickly recalculated as the inputs or assumptions changed. Lodish reported that salespeople were quite comfortable using the system after a single day of training. The data the system required were straightforward. To assess costs, salespeople were asked to input the time it took to make calls in different geographic regions. To estimate the response function in a given account, salespeople were asked to input the minimum and maximum number of calls that could be made in a given preset period (typically one to three months) and to estimate various returns from different calling levels, which captured the salesperson's expert knowledge.

To make the system easier to use, salespeople could estimate the response functions in various ways. The expected returns could be directly given for all possible calling levels in each account; for example, if the minimum number of calls was three and the maximum number was ten, the salesperson could directly estimate the returns from each of the eight different calling levels (3, 4, 5, 6, 7, 8, 9, or 10 calls). Alternatively, the salesperson could ask the computer to generate a best-fitting response curve based on his or her answers to a handful of questions for each account (e.g., "What would the response be if you made zero calls in this account?" "If you made the maximum number of calls?"). Figure 1.1 illustrates some fitted response curves.

Then, the computer developed a calling policy that maximized returns subject to constraints on the required number of calls in each account and on the available time an individual could work. The computations took less than 1 minute in 1971, and the program would easily provide instantaneous feedback today.

Results. In his study, Lodish (1971) reported results for eight Pennwalt salespeople who used CALLPLAN for five months. From the questionnaires of the salespeople and their managers and his own observations, Lodish concluded that the system fostered clearer and more consistent thinking about the calling patterns. Salespeople thought about trade-offs they had not previously considered, and the system fostered better communication between salespeople and their managers. Areas of disagreement on assumptions became explicit after CALLPLAN was used. Furthermore, salespeople bought into the results because the system used their own estimates as inputs for its calculations. In some cases, CALLPLAN helped salespeople maintain a commitment to keep calling on prospects who (in the sense of expected returns) were the best place to spend their limited time. The system became a motivational tool.

Lodish also found that CALLPLAN was better suited to situations in which the selling was repetitive, as he found in plastics, dental equipment, and refrigerants. The amount of time spent selling in an account was an important factor in predicting sales in these cases. Most participants anticipated increases of between 5% and 30%, and

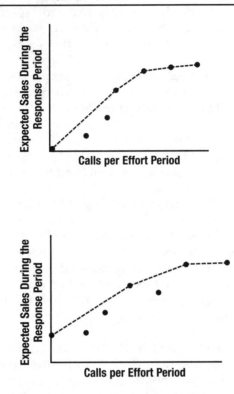

Source: Lodish, Leonard M. (1971), "CALLPLAN: An Interactive Salesman's Call Planning System," *Management Science*, 18 (4), 25–40. Reprinted with permission from the Institute for Operations Research and Management Sciences.

two salespeople reported actual increases of 15% and 30% from more efficient time allocation. Four vacuum cleaner salespeople tried CALLPLAN for four months without much success. Sales in this situation were one-time occurrences, and success was believed to be due to factors other than effort in this case; thus, CALLPLAN was not useful in helping them allocate their time.

In a subsequent study, Fudge and Lodish (1977) designed an experiment to test the effectiveness of CALLPLAN using 20 United Airlines salespeople in New York and San Francisco. The 10 salespeople who used the system were initially skeptical of its worth but viewed it as a productive planning tool afterward. Furthermore,

CALLPLAN produced behavioral changes in these salespeople that led to significantly higher results. After six months of use, the sales results for salespeople using CALLPLAN were 8.1% higher on average than they were for salespeople who did not use the system. The actual dollar improvement for the 10 salespeople was well into the seven figures, and the probability that such an increase occurred by chance alone was only 2.5%.

The decision calculus approach has been used in contexts other than sales force planning. For example, Little and Lodish (1969) developed an early, interactive computer program, called MEDIAC, to help managers select and schedule advertising media. In this system, the user supplied subjective and objective data about media options and the target audience as well as the firm's advertising budget. Using these data, the system scheduled a set of media options that maximized the total market response. Little (1975a, b) developed BRANDAID to help managers make better decisions with regard to their total marketing plan. Analysis of each marketing element (e.g., price, promotion, advertising, distribution) was contained in its own submodule, and each submodule could be expanded on or dropped as the situation required. An advantage of these early systems (and one of the reasons we chose to highlight Lodish's work) was that managers could understand their basic logic even if they did not understand their mathematical algorithms. Thus, working with the system fostered a constructive dialogue among users, and managers were more willing to trust the results. This approach to decision making might prove to be especially useful in new media planning because it is unknown how well the established econometric results in the old media will transfer to the new.

Although we have not highlighted Little's BRANDAID system in depth, we should note that it more commonly uses what-if analysis instead of optimization to complete Stage 2 analysis. This, however, seems to be a minor distinction between it and Lodish's CALLPLAN because both systems are used interactively to make decisions. Managers continually revisit and revise their assumptions while using the system, and this process ultimately leads them to consider what would happen under new scenarios. Models based on decision calculus might be best thought of as providing a direction for improvement in an ever-changing environment.

More recent work has focused on developing computerized systems, known as decision support systems, which are able to integrate a wide variety of information, including managerial judgment, to estimate demand. These systems contain data that are collected in a number of ways; for example, they may include sales and costs data from company records, subjective judgments about what would occur from increased marketing spending, and a database of competitors' products and sales. Various Stage 1 techniques, including decision calculus and econometric models, are used to bring this information together. In a recent decision support systems application, Divakar, Ratchford, and Shankar (2005) developed CHAN4CAST to forecast sales of consumer packaged goods at PepsiCo. Their system allows managers to forecast sales across several channels and to simulate what would happen given a variety of spending and competitive response scenarios. Reinforcing the idea that the system was supposed to be used interactively, CHAN4CAST included a scorecard to track how well past forecasts had predicted the future, and managers could use this scorecard to improve the accuracy of their predictions. PepsiCo estimated that the system would return benefits of more than 1000% of its costs.

Econometric Estimation (Stage 1) and Optimization (Stage 2)

In this section, we highlight two econometric studies that have been coupled with optimization techniques to manage marketing investments made in different phases of the customer life cycle. In the first study, Steenburgh, Ainslie, and Engebretson (2003) develop a method that helps firms decide which customers to acquire. In the second study, Tirenni and colleagues (2007) develop a method that helps firms decide which of their existing customers should be targeted in loyalty program campaigns.

Which Customers to Acquire

Problem. Acquiring the right set of customers is difficult for any company to accomplish, but it can be especially challenging in the context of direct marketing. Companies typically possess limited information that can help predict how prospects will respond to offers, and acquiring third-party data, which often seems of dubious quality, is costly. Furthermore, even when companies can and do choose to buy additional information, the data can be aggregated (e.g., to the zip code level) to protect consumer privacy, a practice that creates additional econometric headaches for analysts. Combined, these factors lead to low rates of consumer response, with success rates commonly being less than 1%. Thus, companies would like to (1) develop methods that make the best use of whatever data they have, (2) find optimal methods for choosing which individual prospects to target, and (3) develop methods that can help them value the data they decide to purchase in terms of dollars.

Approach. Steenburgh, Ainslie, and Engebretson (2003) developed a hierarchical Bayes variance components (HBVC) demand model to solve these problems. Their technique integrates data collected from multiple sources and econometrically models each set of data at the appropriate level of aggregation. They show that traditional techniques, which do not account for different levels of aggregation (e.g., one source being tracked at the individual level and another at the zip code level), result in overly confident parameter estimates and lead to inferior predictions about which prospects should be targeted. Another advantage of their technique is that it allows the zip codes themselves to be used as explanatory variables in the demand model. The old maxim "birds of a feather flock together" holds true, because they show that the zip codes contain useful information about how the people who reside in them behave.

Bayesian models are gaining popularity in the managerial sciences because they can be easily combined with decision theory analysis to improve managerial decisions. In our parlance, Bayesian methods allow a seamless integration of the econometric demand estimation in Stage 1 and the economic optimization in Stage 2. Steenburgh, Ainslie, and Engebretson developed several decision rules based on different relationships between the marginal costs of contacting more prospects and the marginal benefits from having more positive responses, and they show how to implement these decision rules using the Stage 1 results. They show that the decision rules can be relatively easy to implement even when the relationship between costs and benefits is complex.

Results. In an application of their method, Steenburgh, Ainslie, and Engebretson (2003) studied how a private, southern U.S. university should assess its prospects at the inquiry stage of the admissions process. Prospects at this point of the process have requested information about the university but have not yet decided to apply. Steenburgh, Ainslie, and Engebretson used one set of 38,000 prospects to build the demand model and a different set of 34,000 prospects to test the model's predictions. The prospective students resided in approximately 7000 zip codes and declared an interest in 128 different majors. These "massively categorical" variables[5] were directly included as explanatory variables in the HBVC models. Campus visitation data collected at the individual level and supplementary demographic data collected at the zip code level were also used to estimate the models.

Steenburgh, Ainslie, and Engebretson show that their HBVC demand model predicts the enrollment decisions of individual prospects better than the standard model. No matter what data were used to estimate the models, the HBVC model outperformed the null model when the same set of information was used. Indeed, the HBVC models estimated without the supplementary demographic data outperformed the corresponding null models with these data. This suggests that using superior modeling techniques can be more important than purchasing more information. More important than the overall fit of the models, Steenburgh, Ainslie, and Engebretson show that the HBVC model provided a better ordering of the prospects than the null model. The ability of the models to order the prospects was crucial because the ordering helped determine which prospects to target.

Receiver operator curves were used to assess how well the models ordered the prospects (see Figure 1.2). These charts were constructed by repeatedly dividing the prospects into two groups according to their estimated probability of enrollment. Prospects with probabilities below a given cutoff point were placed in one group, and prospects with probabilities above the cutoff point were placed in the other. After this is done for all cutoff points between zero and one, the number of enrollees not selected is graphed against the number of enrollees selected for each division. Visually, this implies that the better the model, the more the curve will move toward the bottom-left-hand corner of the chart. From the figure, it is immediately clear that the HBVC model (represented by the solid line) provides a better ordering of the prospects than the null model (dotted line), no matter what information was used to estimate the models.

In addition to being statistically superior to the null model, the HBVC model helped make a practical difference in the university's ability to target individual prospects. Steenburgh, Ainslie, and Engebretson derived a willingness-to-pay measure to estimate the economic impact both of buying additional data and of using different models. Averaged over an array of financial assumptions, the expected loss from using the null model instead of the HBVC model was 43.6%. This loss was greatest when the university had the least amount of data on which to base its predictions (e.g., when no campus visitation data were present), which suggests, as we might expect, that finding the right model becomes increasingly important when less information is available for analysis.

Which Existing Customers to Target

Problem. Frequent-flier programs have become ubiquitous among all airlines. Most airlines offer elite status to their customers according to how frequently customers fly with them. Typically, airlines consider the upper tier of their frequent-flier programs their most valuable cus-

Figure 1.2 ♦ Receiver Operator Curves Chart Comparing the HBVC and Null Models

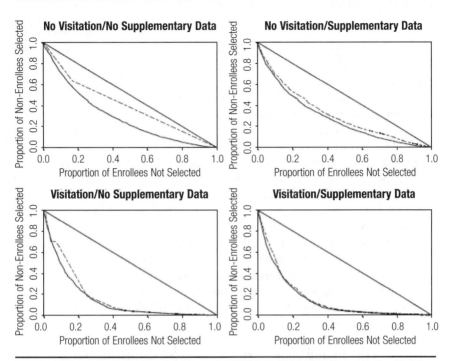

Notes: These four receiver operator curves charts compare the HBVC model with the null model, assuming four different sets of information. In each chart, the HBVC model is graphed with the solid line, and the null model is graphed with the dotted line. Models that better order prospects move toward the lower-left-hand corner of the chart.

Source: Steenburgh, Thomas J., Andrew Ainslie, and Peder Hans Engebretson (2003), "Massively Categorical Variables: Revealing the Information in Zip Codes," *Marketing Science,* 22 (1), 40–57. Reprinted with permission from the Institute for Operations Research and Management Sciences.

tomer segment. Customers in the same elite level (e.g., platinum) receive the same marketing campaign and service. However, customers who accumulate the most miles may not pay the highest fare and may be very costly to serve. How should an airline assess the long-term profitability of its customers, and how should it allocate its marketing resources across these customer groups?

Approach. Tirenni and colleagues (2007) address this question for Finnair. This leading European airline conducts numerous marketing campaigns targeting more than 700,000 customers. A typical customer receives dozens of campaigns each year. These campaigns have differ-ent goals, such as cross- and up-selling, minimizing attrition, and tier upgrading. Campaigns are delivered through various channels, such as mailings, in-cabin brochures, magazines, and the Internet.

In the first stage, Tirenni and colleagues built a Markov decision process, which consists of a set of states, actions, transition probabili-ties, and value functions. For example, a new customer may represent the first state, S_1. A marketing action such as a special offer may move this customer to the second state, S_2 (e.g., repeat purchase), with a transition probability of .7. A club membership may further transition this customer to the third state, S_3 (e.g., loyal customer), with a proba-bility of .6. Various states and actions are obtained from historical data. Transition probabilities are estimated using a Bayesian proce-dure. Customer values are also obtained from the observed data. Given these estimates, future customer dynamics are simulated for a given time horizon (e.g., 12 months) to get a distribution of future val-ues. This provides a mean or expected value as well as variance of customer value.

In the second stage, Tirenni and colleagues set up an optimization problem in which the objective was to maximize the cumulative expected value while minimizing the variance. They further added user-defined budgets and other constraints. This optimization prob-lem was solved using dynamic programming. The solution provided the optimal number of customers to be targeted in each state.

Results. Tirenni and colleagues (2007) applied their model to a sam-ple of 10,000 customers of Finnair using two years of their historical data. Figure 1.3 shows how the optimal policy differs from the histori-cal policy for customers in state S_3 (states are defined on the basis of recency, frequency, monetary value, and statistical procedure). The optimal policy suggests sending no campaigns to approximately 60% of the customers in state S_3, compared with only 25% under the his-torical policy. Figure 1.4 shows the expected long-term value from these customers based on the historical and optimal policy. The opti-mal policy outperforms the shortsighted historical policy. Implementation of this value-based management at Finnair resulted in a greater than 20% reduction in marketing costs as well as response rates that improved by up to 10%.

◆ CONCLUSIONS

Marketing has been, and continues to be, a combination of art and science. With the increasing availability of data and sophistication in

Figure 1.3 ♦ Historical and Optimal Marketing Resource Allocation for Customers in State S_3

From historical . . .   **. . . To optimal**

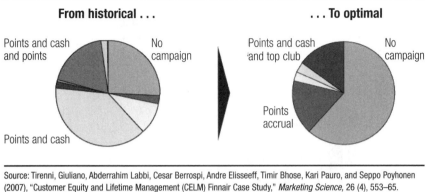

Source: Tirenni, Giuliano, Abderrahim Labbi, Cesar Berrospi, Andre Elisseeff, Timir Bhose, Kari Pauro, and Seppo Poyhonen (2007), "Customer Equity and Lifetime Management (CELM) Finnair Case Study," *Marketing Science*, 26 (4), 553–65. Reprinted with permission from the Institute for Operations Research and Management Sciences.

methods, it is now possible to allocate marketing resources more judiciously. In this chapter, we discussed a two-stage process in which a model of demand is estimated in Stage 1 and its estimates are used as inputs in an optimization model in Stage 2. We proposed a 3×3 matrix, with three different approaches for each of these two stages and discussed pros and cons of these methods. We also highlighted these methods with various applications.

What has been the impact of these advances? Scores of studies in this area now allow us to generalize empirically about the impact of marketing actions on sales and profits. For example, many studies have concluded that the average advertising elasticity is .1, and it is almost twice as much for new products (Assmus, Farley, and Lehmann 1984; Lodish et al. 1995). Similarly, from a series of studies, Gupta and Zeithaml (2006) conclude that one point improvement in customer satisfaction can potentially lead to gains of $240 million to $275 million in firm value. These are important and powerful conclusions that are based not on a single study or a single product category, but rather are broad-based results based on several studies, products, and industries. This level of generalization builds confidence in our understanding of the impact of marketing actions on company performance.

The impact of these studies goes beyond a theoretical understanding of the phenomena. In practical terms, we have witnessed a significant impact at all levels of organization. Studies such as Steenburgh, Ainslie, and Engebretson's (2003) and Jedidi, Mela, and Gupta's

Figure 1.4 ♦ Expected Long-Term Value Using the Historical and Optimal Policy

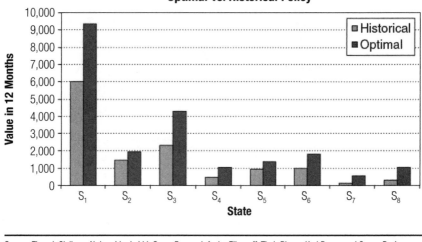

Optimal vs. Historical Policy

Source: Tirenni, Giuliano, Abderrahim Labbi, Cesar Berrospi, Andre Elisseeff, Timir Bhose, Kari Pauro, and Seppo Poyhonen (2007), "Customer Equity and Lifetime Management (CELM) Finnair Case Study," *Marketing Science,* 26 (4), 553–65. Reprinted with permission from the Institute for Operations Research and Management Sciences.

(1999) can help marketing managers improve budget allocation for a brand. Knott, Hayes, and Neslin (2002) use a field test to show that decisions based on their model of cross-selling produce an ROI of 530% for a bank, compared with –17% based on current practices of the bank. Thomas, Reinartz, and Kumar (2004) show that when budgets are allocated as per their model of customer lifetime value, a pharmaceutical company should spend 30% more on marketing to improve its profits by more than 35%, while a catalog retailer should cut its marketing spending by approximately 30% to gain profit improvements of 29%.

Harrah's Entertainment provides perhaps the best example of the impact of this thinking on firm performance. Harrah's drove its entire business strategy based on marketing analytics by understanding and predicting customer behavior through database analysis and experimentation. Harrah's stock price has skyrocketed from under $16 in 1999 to more than $88 in January 2008. Harrah's chief executive officer, Gary Loveman, credits Harrah's enormous success to this relentless pursuit of perfection in which decisions are based on models of consumer behavior rather than on hunch or judgment.

NOTES

1. Scanner data collect information about consumers' store purchases. The data also include information on consumer demographics and complete marketing mix information on all competitive brands.
2. Tremor Web site, "Vocalpoint Panel," (accessed October 2007), [available at http://business.tremor.com//tremor_vocalpoint_panel.html].
3. Tremor Web site, "Tremor Teen Panel," (accessed October 2007), [available at http://business.tremor.com//tremor_teen_panel.html].
4. Split-cable experiments allow advertisers to stream different advertisements to different households in the same city. Purchases of these households are then tracked through store scanners to link the impact of the advertising budget or creative on households' purchase behavior.
5. Steenburgh, Ainslie, and Engebretson (2003) use the term "massively categorical" to describe categorical variables, such as zip codes and majors, that take on many possible values.

REFERENCES

Advertising Age (2007), "100 Leading National Advertisers," (June 25), (accessed March 3, 2008), [available at http://adage.com/datacenter/article?article_id=118652].

Anderson, Eric and Duncan Simester (2004), "Long Run Effects of Promotion Depth on New Versus Established Customers: Three Field Studies," *Marketing Science*, 23 (1), 4–20.

Assmus, Gert, John W. Farley, and Donald R. Lehmann (1984), "How Advertising Affects Sales: Meta-Analysis of Econometric Results," *Journal of Marketing Research*, 21 (February), 65–74.

Blattberg, Robert C. and Stephen J. Hoch (1990), "Database Models and Managerial Intuition, 50% Model + 50% Manager," *Management Science*, 36 (8), 887–99.

Bughin, Jacques, Christoph Erbenich, and Amy Shenkan (2007), "How Companies Are Marketing Online: A McKinsey Global Survey," *The McKinsey Quarterly*, (September).

Direct Marketing Association (2000), *State of the Catalog Industry Report.* New York: Direct Marketing Association.

Divakar, Suresh, Brian T. Ratchford, and Venkatesh Shankar (2005), "CHAN4CAST: A Multichannel Multiregion Forecasting Model for Consumer Packaged Goods," *Marketing Science*, 24 (3), 333–50.

Duvvuri, Sri Devi, Asim Ansari, and Sunil Gupta (2007), "Consumers' Price Sensitivity Across Complementary Categories," *Management Science*, 53 (12), 1933–45.

Eastlack, Joseph O., Jr., and Ambar G. Rao (1986), "Modeling Response to Advertising and Pricing Changes for 'V-8' Cocktail Vegetable Juice," *Marketing Science*, 5 (Summer), 245–59.

Eisenstein, Eric M. and Leonard M. Lodish (2002), "Precisely Worthwhile or Vaguely Worthless: Are Marketing Decision Support and Intelligent Systems 'Worth It'?" in *Handbook of Marketing*, Barton Weitz and Robin Wensley, eds. London: Sage Publications.

Fudge, William K. and Leonard M. Lodish (1977), "Evaluation of the Effectiveness of a Model Based Salesman's Planning System by Field Experimentation," *Interfaces*, 8 (1, Part 2), 97–106.

Godes, David and Dina Mayzlin (2007), "Firm-Created Word-of-Mouth Communication: Evidence from a Field Test," working paper, Harvard Business School.

Granovetter, Mark S. (1973), "The Strength of Weak Ties," *The American Journal of Sociology*, 78 (May), 1360–80.

Guadagni, Peter M. and John D.C. Little (1983), "A Logit Model of Brand Choice Calibrated on Scanner Data," *Marketing Science*, 2 (3), 203–208.

Gupta, Sunil (1988), "Impact of Sales Promotions on When, What, and How Much to Buy," *Journal of Marketing Research*, 25 (November), 342–56.

———, Dominique Hanssens, Bruce Hardie, Wiliam Kahn, V. Kumar, Nathaniel Lin, Nalini Ravishanker, and S. Sriram (2006), "Modeling Customer Lifetime Value," *Journal of Service Research*, 9 (2), 139–55.

——— and Valarie Zeithaml (2006), "Customer Metrics and Their Impact on Financial Performance," *Marketing Science*, 25 (6), 718–39.

Jedidi, Kamel, Carl F. Mela, and Sunil Gupta (1999), "Managing Advertising and Promotion for Long-Run Profitability," *Marketing Science*, 18 (1), 1–22.

Knott, Aaron, Andrew Hayes, and Scott Neslin (2002), "Next-Product-to-Buy Model for Cross-Selling Applications," *Journal of Interactive Marketing*, 16 (3), 59–75.

Kumar, V., J. Andrew Petersen, and Robert P. Leone (2007), "How Valuable Is Word of Mouth?" *Harvard Business Review*, 85 (October), 139–46.

Lilien, Gary L., Philip Kotler, and K. Sridhar Moorthy (1992), *Marketing Models*. Englewood Cliffs, NJ: Prentice Hall.

Little, John D.C. (1970), "Models and Managers: The Concept of Decision Calculus," *Management Science*, 16 (8), B466–B485.

——— (1975a), "BRANDAID: A Marketing-Mix Model, Part 1: Structure," *Operations Research*, 23 (4), 628–55.

——— (1975b), "BRANDAID: A Marketing-Mix Model, Part 2: Implementation, Calibration, and Case Study," *Operations Research*, 23 (4), 656–73.

——— and Leonard M. Lodish (1969), "A Media Planning Calculus," *Operations Research*, 17 (1), 1–35.

Lodish, Leonard M. (1971), "CALLPLAN: An Interactive Salesman's Call Planning System," *Management Science*, 18 (4, Part II), 25–40.

———, Magid Abraham, Stuart Kalmenson, Jeanne Livelsberger, Beth Lubetken, Bruce Richardson, and Mary Ellen Stevens (1995), "How T.V. Advertising Works: A Meta-Analysis of 389 Real World Split Cable T.V. Advertising Experiments," *Journal of Marketing Research*, 32 (May), 125–39.

Loveman, Gary (2003), "Diamonds in the Data Mine," *Harvard Business Review*, 81 (May), 2–6.

Manchanda, Puneet, Asim Ansari, and Sunil Gupta (1999), "The 'Shopping Basket': A Model for Multi-Category Purchase Incidence Decisions," *Marketing Science*, 18 (2), 95–114.

Mantrala, Murali (2006), "Allocating Marketing Resources," in *The Handbook of Marketing*, Barton A. Weitz and Robin Wensley, eds. Thousand Oaks, CA: Sage Publications.

Mela, Carl F., Sunil Gupta, and Donald R. Lehmann (1997), "The Long-Term Impact of Promotions and Advertising on Consumer Brand Choice," *Journal of Marketing Research*, 34 (May), 248–61.

Natter, Martin, Thomas Reutterer, Andreas Mild, and Alfred Taudes (2007), "An Assortmentwide Decision-Support System for Dynamic Pricing and Promotion Planning in DIY Retailing," *Marketing Science*, 26 (4), 576–83.

Pauwels, K., S. Siddarth, and D.M. Hanssens (2002), "The Long-Term Effects of Pricing and Promotions on Category Traffic, Brand Choice, and Purchase Quantity," *Journal of Marketing Research*, 39 (November), 421–39.

Sinha, Prabhakant and Andris A. Zoltner (2001), "Sales-Force Decision Models: Insights from 25 years of Implementation," *Interfaces*, 31 (3, Part 2 of 2), S8–S44.

Steenburgh, Thomas J. (2007), "Measuring Consumer and Competitive Impact with Elasticity Decompositions," *Journal of Marketing Research*, 44 (November), 636–46.

———, Andrew Ainslie, and Peder Hans Engebretson (2003), "Massively Categorical Variables: Revealing the Information in Zip Codes," *Marketing Science*, 22 (1), 40–57.

Tellis, Gerard J. (1988), "The Price Elasticity of Selective Demand: A Meta-Analysis of Econometric Models of Sales," *Journal of Marketing Research*, 25 (November), 331–41.

Thomas, Jacquelyn, Werner Reinartz, and V. Kumar (2004), "Getting the Most Out of Your Customers," *Harvard Business Review*, 82 (July–August), 116–23.

Tirenni, Giuliano, Abderrahim Labbi, Cesar Berrospi, Andre Elisseeff, Timir Bhose, Kari Pauro, and Seppo Poyhonen (2007), "Customer Equity and Lifetime Management (CELM) Finnair Case Study," *Marketing Science*, 26 (4), 553–65.

Venkatesan, R. and V. Kumar (2004), "A Customer Lifetime Value Framework for Customer Selections and Resource Allocation Strategy," *Journal of Marketing*, 68 (October), 106–125.

Wierenga, Berend, Gerrit H. Van Bruggen, and Richard Staelin (1999), "The Success of Marketing Management Support Systems," *Marketing Science*, 18 (3), 196–207.

Wittink, Dick R. (2002), "Analysis of ROI for Pharmaceutical Promotion (ARPP)," white paper presentation to the Association of Medical Publications, (September 18), (accessed February 11, 2008), [available at http://www.vioworks.com/clients/amp/].

PART TWO

MARKETING MIX RESOURCE ALLOCATION AND PLANNING IN PRACTICE

How can companies better understand how well their marketing investments achieve intended business goals and objectives? The two chapters in Part Two address this broad question.

In Chapter 2, "Marketing Effectiveness: Practical Approaches to Measurement and Management," Gordon Wyner of Millward Brown describes three common ways for measuring marketing effectiveness. These include (1) "top-down" analyses of the impact of marketing mix elements on market performance over time, (2) "bottom-up" approaches to understanding the value of customers, and (3) methods for understanding the effect of individual marketing and communication levers.

Wyner points out that achieving marketing effectiveness requires several distinct activities, only one of which is analysis. That is, the organization must be prepared to receive and act on analytical results to realize the full benefits. Often this requires creating a common understanding of how marketing works for the company and achieving consensus on the strategic intent of marketing investments.

Wyner emphasizes that marketing effectiveness is more of a disciplined process than a particular answer to a business question. It calls for assimilating ideas that are new to the organization, which may run counter to traditional ways of thinking. The analytical outputs of the process need to be continuously monitored to ensure that performance is actually improving and to identify new opportunities for sustaining and increasing it over time.

In Chapter 3, Todd Powers and Anil Menon from IBM detail their company's programmatic approach to advertising research. Their article, "Practical Measurement of Advertising Impact: The IBM Experience," describes the work of IBM's Market Intelligence Center of Excellence related to optimizing IBM investments in advertising around the world and across various media, including television, print, interactive, and out-of-home media outlets.

A unique feature of IBM's approach to advertising research is the focus on tying revenue (or the lack thereof) directly to specific advertising campaigns. Powers and Menon systematically document IBM's pioneering research program that isolates the direct effect of ad exposure on sales revenue, as well as effects on critical stages in the purchase funnel, including ad awareness, brand perceptions, propensity to buy, lead generation, and conversion. Insights garnered from this research program have paid huge dividends in refining marketing resource allocation decisions at IBM.

Taken together, these two articles offer a rare glimpse into the practical aspects of marketing mix resource allocation and planning. In doing so, they place marketing analytics in the broader domain of marketing accountability.

CHAPTER 2

MARKETING EFFECTIVENESS: PRACTICAL APPROACHES TO MEASUREMENT AND MANAGEMENT

Gordon Wyner, Millward Brown Inc.

◆ OPPORTUNITY

How do firms allocate marketing resource investments to meet their objectives? The answer is a complex one. In some ways, this is the most critical of marketing decisions. It's where firms take action to fund certain programs, people, and long-term plans. It's where companies decide what levers to use to compete with the full range of competitors, across their entire portfolio of products and services, channels, and customer segments.

Resource allocation decisions require that firms have knowledge of the relationship between marketing investments and business performance. This involves understanding the extent to which previously made expenditures have (or haven't) achieved their financial goals. Sound allocation decisions require that marketers use knowledge of how previous investments have worked to plan for future marketing initiatives and to make investments to support them. In other words, resource allocation and planning justifies both past and future actions.

Linking marketing and finance has become a priority for most companies over the past ten years. Studies by industry organizations consistently indicate that doing so is a very high business priority, whether the focus is on marketing productivity or effectiveness, investment decision making, financial accountability, or return on marketing. Over the past decade, the member companies of the Marketing Science Institute have consistently voted the link between marketing and finance among their highest priorities, and their focus and work shows the evolving importance of marketing accountability to practitioners and the ways new knowledge continues to be developed in this area.

At the same time, there continues to be concern that marketing isn't yet delivering as much value as it should. The CMO Council (2008) reports that though an increasing number of companies expect to begin marketing effectiveness initiatives, more than half of them still don't track the necessary metrics. There are numerous examples of the magnitude of the opportunity for marketers to benefit from a greater link to financial outcomes. The following are typical of what is found in practice:

♦ Optimizing the marketing mix can achieve financial improvements of 10%–20%.

♦ Brand value accounts for 30% of earnings.

♦ 20% of customers account for 80% of profits.

♦ A majority of customers are unprofitable to serve.

♦ "Good" versus "average" advertising can produce percentage-point increases in market share.

♦ Experimental testing across multiple mix variables can double yields.

There is plenty of opportunity, but the perception remains that the challenge of marketing accountability has yet to be solved. The increased availability of analytical software and decision-support tools provides some hope that the problem is solvable. Today, companies are using marketing science to deploy marketing resources more effectively to satisfy the performance and growth requirements of owners and shareholders.

Companies also have an opportunity to increase the efficiency of their resource utilization by reducing spending on activities that are not as productive as they could be. This might mean directly cutting a budget for, say, television advertising or creating more efficient processes that allow marketers to create better advertising copy, target customers more effectively, or purchase media space for less cost.

◆ REAL-WORLD ISSUES

What are the challenges to achieving an adequate return on marketing? There are many; some have been with us for a long time, and changing aspects of the current marketing environment drive others.

The Long Run Versus the Short Run

How long does it take for the effects of marketing investments to take hold, and how long do they last? The time paths of some marketing investments are understood better than others. The traditional advertising vehicles of television, radio, and print are fairly well understood. The relationship between gross rating points (GRPs) expended and consumer response in terms of awareness and purchase behavior has been modeled for decades. Similarly, exposure to magazine and print advertising is well understood through sophisticated models of audience accumulation and segmentation.

Less is known about new media, such as Internet display and search advertising. Although there are continuing improvements in modeling each of these new stimuli individually, there is less progress in modeling them in an integrated way along with the traditional vehicles.

More important, there is a huge and ongoing struggle between the need for short-term business performance (which public companies require for quarterly visibility) and the long-term buildup of marketing assets, such as brand and customer equity, base sales, and repeat purchases. The financial imperative of making marketing pay back in time frames that the external market (e.g., shareholders, stock purchasers) can comprehend is pushing the science of understanding how marketing works.

The irony is that longer-term effects, though more difficult to measure, are often more valuable. It's relatively easy, for example, to measure the short-term impact of direct response to television ads or direct-mail promotions and incremental sales response to advertising and promotion activities. It's more difficult, however, to accurately measure an increase in brand value (e.g., the net present value [NPV] of brand cash flows) or an increase in customer lifetime value (e.g., the NPV of customer cash flows).

In mature consumer products categories, in general, it is agreed that long-term effects have twice the magnitude of short-term effects. Therefore, because the overall return on investment (ROI) of advertising can hinge on these long-term effects, any systematic program for marketing effectiveness should address both short and long time frames.

Proliferation

With the dramatic proliferation of marketing channels, media vehicles, and product offerings (Figure 2.1), how is a firm to know where to focus marketing resources for the best advantage? The question of resource allocation calls for more than an understanding of how each marketing investment works by itself over time. It requires an understanding of how the various elements work together, reinforce one another, or even perhaps work against one another. For example, can promotional cash incentives (e.g., grocery coupons, cash-back incentives, "free" wireless minutes) undermine a brand's position and customers' loyalty? How do digital media (e.g., Internet-enabled advertising and search) work in combination with these other variables to reinforce the marketing strategy?

Active Consumers

Consumers and customers have become more active and empowered in the marketing process thanks to the proliferation of choices available to them, the technologies that enable them to communicate and make their demands known (e.g., search, blogs, Web configurators, other purchasing sites), and some active resistance to marketing messages. Do the traditional rules about marketing spend and allocation apply when the consumer does the "deciding" or even just participates in "cogeneration" along with the marketer?

Many of the tools for analyzing marketing effectiveness suggest a straightforward cause-and-effect relationship between marketing investment and customer response. Perhaps this unidirectional view needs updating as manufacturers cede some degree of control of their brands to consumers. In addition, we see more situations in which the consumer decides when to engage with the brand actively, such as through blogs, rather than through passive situations, such as viewing television commercials.

Is History Useful?

How can marketers predict the consequences of future actions by looking at what has happened in the past? Such predictions are especially challenging in a period of rapid technological change, when the present looks less like the past than it did, say, 20 years ago. For many new channels, media, and consumer dynamics, there is no reference point in the past. For example, what is predictive of behavior on social-networking sites? What is predictive of the impact of video downloading on cell phones (which has current penetration of less

Figure 2.1 ♦ Marketing Channels and Technology Expansion: More Complex Marketing
Front and Back Rooms

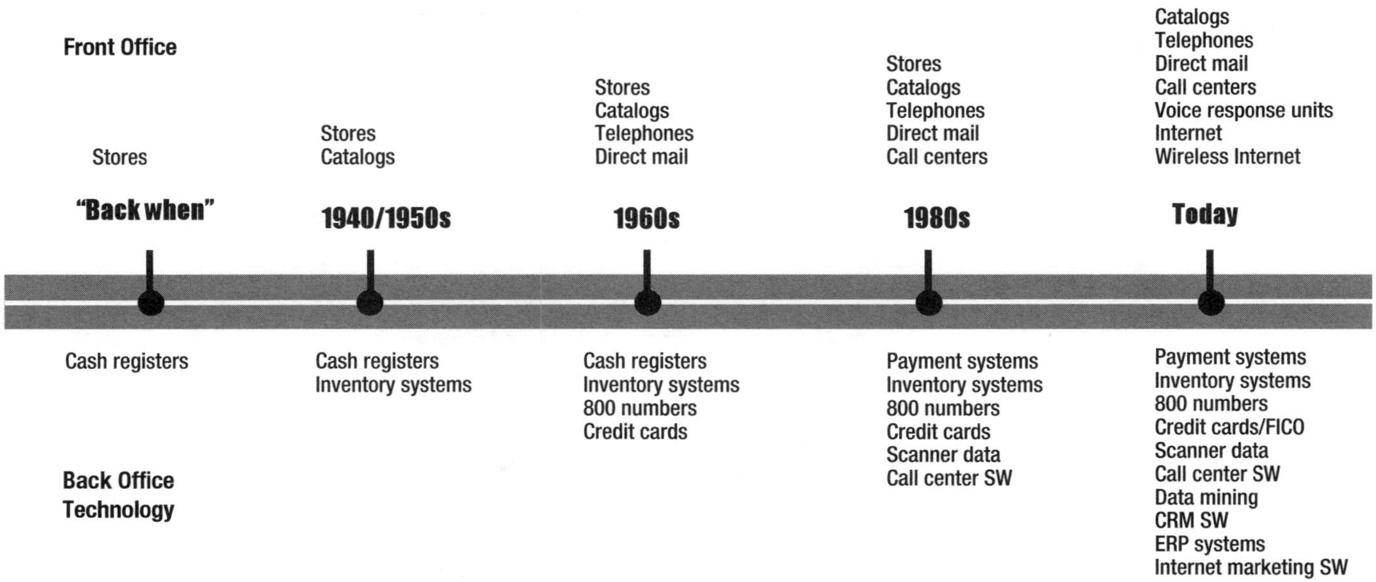

	"Back when"	1940/1950s	1960s	1980s	Today
Front Office					Catalogs
					Telephones
					Direct mail
			Stores	Stores	Call centers
			Catalogs	Catalogs	Voice response units
		Stores	Telephones	Telephones	Internet
	Stores	Catalogs	Direct mail	Direct mail	Wireless Internet
				Call centers	
Back Office Technology					Payment systems
					Inventory systems
					800 numbers
			Cash registers	Payment systems	Credit cards/FICO
			Inventory systems	Inventory systems	Scanner data
		Cash registers	800 numbers	800 numbers	Call center SW
		Inventory systems	Credit cards	Credit cards	Data mining
	Cash registers			Scanner data	CRM SW
				Call center SW	ERP systems
					Internet marketing SW

than 2%)? What is the impact of consumer-controlled blogs that focus on particular brands?

Despite the expansion of new channels, it's important to put into perspective the relative expenditures that firms devote to them. Traditional advertising still accounts for most ad spend and does not appear to be ceding its top spot any time soon (Figure 2.2). It's reasonable to assume that in the future, marketers will find greater use for pilot tests, experiments, and analogies from other media, channels, and markets. Traditional methods for measurement and analysis will continue to be stretched to take into account the emerging marketing stimuli.

Risk

What are the consequences of making mistakes with marketing allocation decisions? What is the downside risk? The usual rules of thumb (e.g., spend what competitors spend, or spend the same as last year) are not likely to serve marketers well going forward. Firms must use a different allocation approach when their options include a more complex mix of traditional, new, and still-emerging channels. Portfolio decisions are more complicated on several dimensions. Consider the combinations of sales channels, media outlets, customer segments, and products that are available to a large consumer products company, automobile manufacturer, or service provider. Some of the uncontrollable factors, such as the seasonality of a product category, are familiar. Others, such as new competitors that come from outside the product category, are relatively new.

How does a firm place its marketing investment bets in an environment of such uncertainty? The answer lies in adopting more disciplined methods for evaluating a diverse set of options on a common basis, in measuring the effectiveness of programs, and in tying marketing spend to financial outcomes.

Assessing risk is an important component of any analysis of marketing effectiveness. Rather than limit the analysis to deterministic methods of linking marketing mix to sales or share, a risk assessment should include additional dynamic measures such as velocity of cash flows, variability of earnings, and NPV, which explicitly take into account the uncertainties of estimated effects.

◆ THE ACTIVITIES OF ACCOUNTABILITY

The aspiration to allocate resources better and to achieve accountability conjures the image of a decision maker standing at the com-

Figure 2.2 ◆ Is History a Good Guide to the Future?

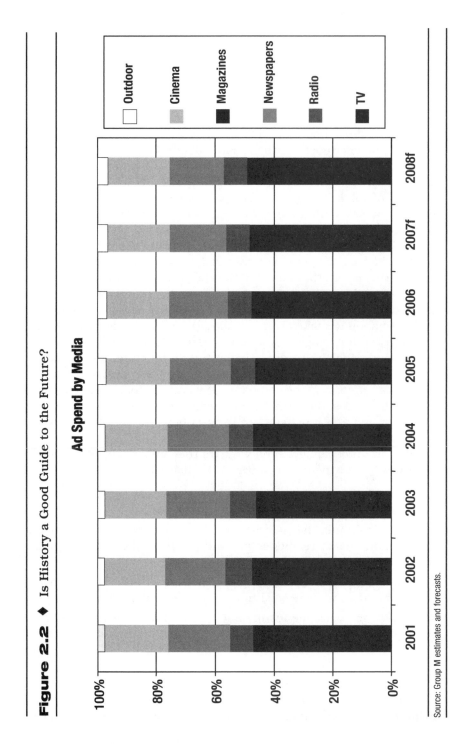

Ad Spend by Media

Legend: Outdoor, Cinema, Magazines, Newspapers, Radio, TV

Source: Group M estimates and forecasts.

pany's control dials and turning the knobs to achieve certain business performance outcomes. He or she consciously and rationally chooses among alternative spend levels and allocations with a particular strategy in mind.

Real decision making, however, isn't quite so clear cut. To be in a position to make informed judgments, the decision maker needs to have an understanding of how marketing investments work—in other words, how they influence customer behavior—which will lead to decisions and responses that ultimately generate revenue and profit for the firm. Having such an understanding requires the ability to orchestrate the activities of all key players inside an organization, outside service providers such as advertising agencies and researchers, and external business partners such as dealers, distributors, and retailers.

Pulling the right levers involves several stages of often overlapping activities. Not all the steps are observed all the time, in practice, and when they do occur, they do not always occur in the same logical order. Still, at a high level, it's useful to break down the process into the steps that lead to the measurement of marketing effectiveness and the use of this information to make decisions about spend levels and allocation.

Given the full range of talent and capabilities that are needed to implement an effective resource management program, it is important that the program include several stages that are organizational in nature (e.g., preparing the company for what's to come, implementing the results) and several that are analytically intensive and draw on interpretations and judgments of various types of data to give direction to the process.

What are those stages, and why are they important? They can be grouped into four main categories:

1. *Align:* Agree on common language and how marketing works and achieve consensus on strategic intent.

2. *Analyze:* Enable the process with data and metrics, understand cause-and-effect relationships, and evaluate alternatives actions and choose.

3. *Adopt:* Translate decisions into specific action steps, procure goods and services needed to act, and implement the plans.

4. *Adapt:* Feed back the results and update the strategy.

We now examine each stage in more detail.

Align

To put the measurement and management of marketing mix resources on a proper foundation, marketers must expend significant effort to prepare the organization for change. An important first step is to align relevant decision makers around how the marketing process works and the strategic intent of marketing activities. The measurement of marketing performance requires a definition of success: What are we trying to accomplish?

Firms have different business models (even firms within the same industry) and different languages to describe them. They often have simple but useful shorthand visual representations that enable disparate units within the organization to talk about marketing effectiveness. The purchase funnel, the strategic cube, and the template of acquisition, development, and retention all reflect different views on how a business works relative to its customer marketing efforts. In different ways, each captures a common set of principles about marketing and offers a framework for strategic intentions. It begins to suggest where the marketing levers under the control of management play a role (Figure 2.3).

This type of vision of the business—how marketing works and the strategic intent of marketing—allows management to think in terms of its accountability in achieving performance levels and in making improvements. Without a clearly defined vision, there is too much room for confusion, distrust among organizational units, and disputes about who is supposed to make things happen.

A financial services company, for example, often used the purchase funnel as its primary visual and conceptual framework to describe how marketing works in its business. However, the operations unit didn't explicitly use this approach, nor did the marketing department, at first. The two groups had much conflict because of their contrasting positions and goals: Operations was highly quantitative and analytical, being closely associated with underwriting and pricing, whereas marketing was limited to advertising theme and copy development. Over time, each group developed a mutual business interest in the success of the other's department. Operations came to understand how the marketing process worked, with advertising serving as the key driver of adding new prospects to the top of the funnel, which in turn led to customer acquisition. The only way for underwriting to have sufficient prospects was through a robust advertising process with clear goals. By agreeing on the structure of this process, the two departments could then agree on business goals and assign appropriate, realistic responsibilities to achieve them.

Some of the distinctions between goals and responsibilities may seem obvious. For example, advertising doesn't close accounts; that requires an interaction with service personnel or online services. Service people, such as branch or call center staff who field inbound

Figure 2.3 ◆ Align: Common Language Often Can Be Visual

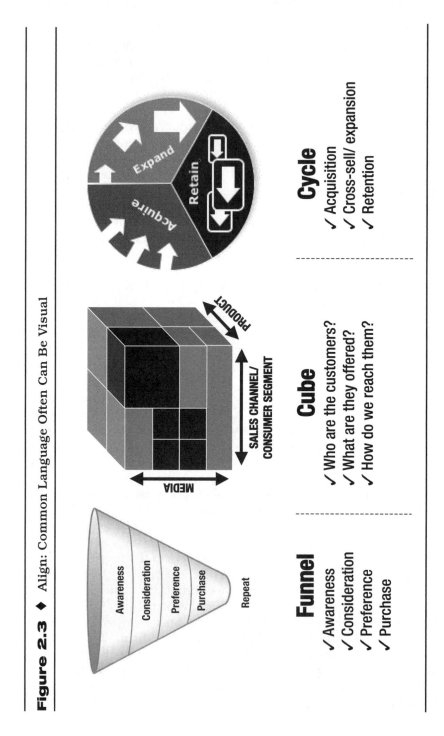

Funnel

✓ Awareness
✓ Consideration
✓ Preference
✓ Purchase

Cube

✓ Who are the customers?
✓ What are they offered?
✓ How do we reach them?

Cycle

✓ Acquisition
✓ Cross-sell/ expansion
✓ Retention

customer inquiries and help set up accounts and may influence the closing of a deal, are not necessarily responsible for bringing in prospects and thus can only work with the leads they are given. Communication bears much of the responsibility for stimulating demand (Figure 2.4).

Analyze

Appropriate, timely, and accurate information to support the decision-making process, such as data streams on prior investments, activities, market response, and financials, enables the analysis of marketing effectiveness. With just a few exceptions, history is a critical part of anticipating future performance.

A starting point is for firms to create metrics from readily available data. Not all businesses have the resources to design measurement systems from the ground up that provide ideal metrics. However, most companies have access to data that they don't even consider the basis for good marketing metrics, including transaction records, financial reports, customer counts (e.g., retail stores' direct observations of traffic), sales calls, service calls, requests for information (by channel), appointment books, product shipments, inventory changes, and the like.

Firms can combine these raw data with marketing inputs (expenditures on things such as direct mail outgo, sales force, and advertising) and financial outputs (information on revenue and profits by business unit over time) to begin building a platform for an evaluation of marketing effectiveness that can support resource decisions (Figure 2.5).

Identifying the metrics, developing a regular measurement and review program, and placing the results into simple scorecards are key steps in the analytical process. By themselves, though, metrics in a scorecard don't address the cause-and-effect relationship between investment inputs and financial outputs. For firms to achieve a deeper understanding, the analysis must associate management actions (e.g., decisions to spend) with outcomes (e.g., customers' behavioral responses that lead to financial results). Without this association, there is no clear attribution of performance changes and no "what-if" capability to generate and test alternative decisions and mix allocations.

The generation and evaluation of alternative potential decision scenarios are conceptually distinct stages in the analytic process. More sophisticated modeling approaches enable analysts to apply the estimated model structure to hypothetical situations in which the nature and level of spending vary. Although there is sometimes a single "optimal" solution (e.g., invest X dollars in marketing, with A percentage to television advertising, B percentage to direct-mail pro-

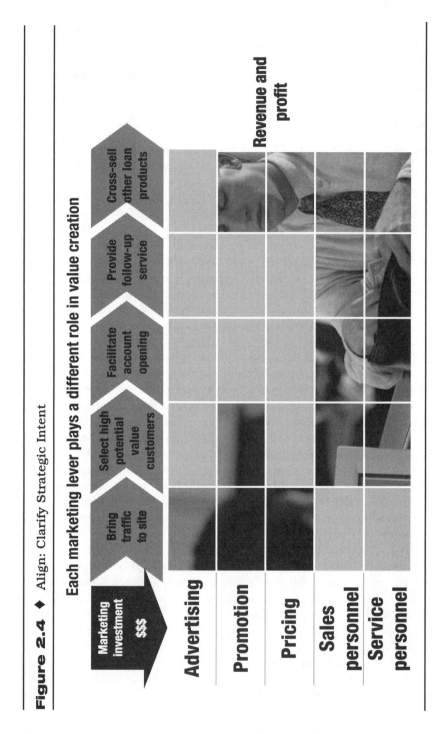

Figure 2.4 ♦ Align: Clarify Strategic Intent

Each marketing lever plays a different role in value creation

	Bring traffic to site	Select high potential value customers	Facilitate account opening	Provide follow-up service	Cross-sell other loan products	
Marketing investment $$$						
Advertising						Revenue and profit
Promotion						
Pricing						
Sales personnel						
Service personnel						

Figure 2.5 ♦ Metrics: How to Measure Financial Input, Customer Response, and Financial Output

Investment Input	Customer Measures	Financial Output
✓ Advertising and promotion	✓ Awareness	✓ Acquisition
	✓ Consideration	✓ Cross-sell
✓ Direct mail	✓ Preference	✓ Wallet share
✓ Channel	✓ Benefits	✓ Retention
✓ Product	✓ Choice/purchase	✓ Revenue
✓ Pricing	✓ Usage	✓ Cost-to-serve
✓ Service	✓ Channel experience	✓ Profit
✓ Loyalty programs	✓ Satisfaction	✓ ...
✓ ...	✓ ...	

Does response vary by segment, geography, channel, competition, and time?

motions, and C percentage to distribution), more often there are multiple feasible alternatives that firms must judge on many criteria before they determine the best option.

An explicit decision about which course to pursue, amid great complexity (e.g., a portfolio of brands, customer segments, and marketing levers), is often based on decision criteria beyond the data and analysis themselves. For example, a global company may want to boost performance in an underdeveloped region for strategic reasons rather than plow most of its investment into its most profitable region. This might require more investment than what the global optimum would allow. If a firm has a fuzzy sense of its decisions and why it made them, it will be difficult to say if the decisions worked and what could be done better in the next round.

Adopt

Analyses alone have no real value until they are applied in an organization. Although this may seem obvious, there are many examples of companies that tabulate and summarize data in various ways but never take the crucial next step of acting on the results. Analyses don't walk off the page into action. Sometimes they are difficult to read and don't give clear implications, which makes it hard to take direction from them. It's useful to break down the execution phases into some of the component steps in which companies translate, procure, and implement plans based on marketing effectiveness analyses.

Translation is the application of the allocation decision to specific activities at the program, person, and plan level. To be effective in the market, the translation must be consistent with the implications of the data and analysis. The quality of the spending (e.g., the effectiveness of advertising) must measure up to what the allocation assumes, or the results will not. For example, the output of a mix allocation analysis might yield recommendations for particular amounts and percentages of total budget to be spent in a certain category, such as advertising, consumer promotion, and trade marketing. What types of advertising messages, media, and promotion programs are compatible with the analysis results? Which of the many trade marketing categories (e.g., sales force, collateral, incentives) should be put in place?

Companies with moderately complex marketing plans will probably carry out analyses at a higher level than the specific program. Moreover, some future programs may be new (i.e., they haven't been tried before), so they must be designed in a way that is compatible with the analytical output and direction.

Procurement of the goods and services that constitute the marketing investments (e.g., advertising media and creative services, databases, distribution expenses) can be a major set of activities on its own. However, such activities are important to include in the discussion of marketing effectiveness for several reasons. For example, the procurement step sometimes occurs on its own schedule and buying process, somewhat independent of the other stages. Consider media buying, which is a function of the market for ad space; in television, for example, the networks determine the schedule for up-front purchasing. The actual purchase price can vary dramatically by advertiser, depending on size (e.g., aggregated purchases across product categories) and sophistication in the buying process (e.g., understanding of media companies' inventory management, use of intermediaries such as media agencies).

Even if an analytical platform of marketing effectiveness provides for changing types and levels of spend, it isn't always possible to make the desired changes in practice. Purchases might have been made in anticipation of their need, sometimes well in advance of the media delivery (e.g., months ahead of the Super Bowl for television ads). The very fact that when and how media purchase (and the purchase of other marketing services) influences the prices paid suggests that the outcome can significantly affect ROI.

For example, consider a prototypical large company with many brands, large media and creative agencies, and the technical resources for ROI analyses. Compare that company with a small company with a single brand, small agencies, and no technical resources.

A single GRP of media exposure may seem to have the same impact in the market for both companies. However, the large company can buy a GRP for less cost, use it more effectively with superior creative development resources, and analyze it better to understand how to improve effectiveness in the next planning cycle. By analogy, a small cookie manufacturer may get less impact from a pound of sugar in its baking process than a larger manufacturer that has more sophisticated equipment that lets it stretch the same ingredient farther. The larger manufacturer probably buys the sugar at a lower price per pound, thus increasing its ROI, than the small manufacturer.

Excellence in execution is receiving more play in the business press as chief executive officers emphasize the importance of doing the work as much or more than coming up with the plan to do the work. This also applies to marketing, which involves many plans that are to be executed with specific programs of advertising, promotion, distribution, and pricing. There can be significant gaps between what is planned and what is actually delivered in the market. A familiar example is in the case of television advertising, in which the advertiser monitors GRP delivery, learns of a gap, and fills it through "make goods." Without accurate execution of the plan, it's difficult or even impossible to evaluate how well a particular ad worked and whether the investment paid back.

Adapt

Learning from marketing effectiveness analyses does not come naturally to companies. They must develop processes to capture explicitly the results of market tests and demonstrations, sample mail drops, and advertising campaigns. This involves documenting from experience what worked and what didn't so that future decisions will improve on past activities.

Some companies collect massive amounts of data but do not adequately analyze that data or ignore them completely. For example, a retail bank went to considerable lengths to design in-market tests for some of its offers and to generate response data. However, there was little forethought about the decision criteria for actions that the bank would later take as a result of the analyses; the tests demonstrated that the offers achieved a certain volume of response, but there was no plan to conduct systematic comparisons against control cells or prior time periods to estimate lift. In other cases, analysts estimated lift but not financial value (i.e., ROI). The bank considered depth of the analyses less important than setting up for the next test to meet budgeted goals for program output.

To improve the use of its information, the bank initiated a rapid prototyping approach for new processes to ensure that results were calculated in a meaningful way and fed back to marketing managers for improvements in the next round of tests. Team leaders were selected according to their understanding of the need for business results, not just measures of throughput or behavioral response. They were given permission to break existing processes that were too slow to provide any meaningful feedback or create faster work-arounds. For their work tasks to be considered complete, marketing managers were required to provide feedback and to recommend strategy modifications. By imposing decision criteria, increasing speed, and mandating feedback, teams were able to develop a far more productive process. They replicated the process for their own projects and were then tasked with training other teams that were just getting started. The goal was to build one team's success on another, which would lead eventually to a new process across the organization.

Ideally, such a feedback process ties in directly to the up-front alignment process. The marketing department's establishment of the strategic intent of marketing initiatives should lead directly to performance measurement improvements (Figure 2.6). It is difficult, but not impossible, for companies to create and sustain these types of processes. Capital One Financial has used rapid, experimental, results-oriented testing to fuel growth in its credit card business. The company's annual report has cited this process, and the thousands of tests it runs annually, as a key success factor.

Although some aspects of the test-and-learn process are easier to implement in direct marketing contexts, the same principles apply to other media and channels, including television advertising. The specific tools are different, but the principles are the same. The costs of creating the test process should be commensurate with the marketing investment. It is possible to keep the accountability process on its own budget.

An important part of a systematic testing process is to keep a cumulative database of results for normative and comparative analysis going forward. This provides a context for evaluating performance. For example, a consumer packaged goods manufacturer used marketing mix modeling to isolate the effects of television advertising on sales for most of its products. Over a three-year period, it tracked about 20 instances of specific ad copy that could be characterized in terms of sales response, cost of campaign, and diagnostic measures such as copy-testing scores and in-market performance on brand metrics. Such data provide a basis for understanding the performance of new campaigns and point to the kinds of changes that the company could

Figure 2.6 ◆ Test and Learn Process

Disciplined approach ensures that new information drives actions.

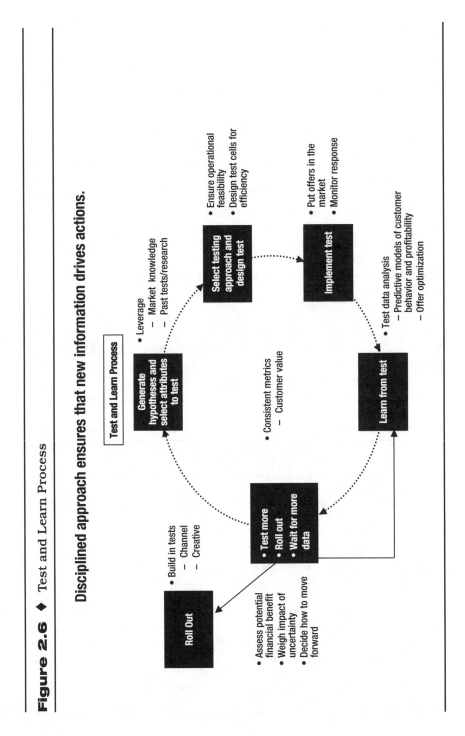

Test and Learn Process

Generate hypotheses and select attributes to test
- Leverage
  - Market knowledge
  - Past tests/research

Select testing approach and design test
- Ensure operational feasibility
- Design test cells for efficiency

Implement test
- Put offers in the market
- Monitor response

Learn from test
- Test data analysis
  - Predictive models of customer behavior and profitability
  - Offer optimization

- Consistent metrics
  - Customer value

Test more
- Test more
- Roll out
- Wait for more data

Roll Out
- Build in tests
  - Channel
  - Creative

- Assess potential financial benefit
- Weigh impact of uncertainty
- Decide how to move forward

make to improve the weight, schedule, and execution for current and future campaigns.

♦ ANALYTICAL APPROACHES

Although there are many analytical approaches and nearly endless varieties that could be important to the marketing effectiveness discipline, I describe three here (Figure 2.7). They reflect my experience as a practitioner, which is based on a broad mix of industries (services, durables, nondurable consumer products, and business-to-business) and mostly large companies that have significant budgets (in the tens of millions of dollars) for outside expenditures on advertising. In general, the same logic, albeit with scaled-down methodological approaches that are commensurate with the company's resources, applies to small companies.

Top-Down Approaches: Marketing Mix Modeling

Marketing mix modeling is intended to quantify the influence of each measurable element of a marketing plan on brand sales over time. Typical plan elements include advertising, promotion, pricing, distribution, and product variations (essentially, the four Ps). Such modeling views the market from a top-down perspective, such as the aggregate U.S. market or a submarket such as the Midwestern states.

Figure 2.7 ♦ Analyze: Different Tools Approach the Problem at Different Levels

---

- **Top Down Approaches: Marketing Mix Modeling**
  - ✓ Quantifies influence of each element of a marketing plan on brand sales over time, e.g. advertising, promotion, pricing, distribution, and product.
  - ✓ Supports resource allocation decisions at the aggregate market level such as the total US or sub-markets

- **Bottom Up Approaches: Customer Valuation**
  - ✓ Quantifies customer value, current and future, to support acquisition, development, and retention
  - ✓ Determines allowable amount of investment, and the channels and vehicles for reaching customers

- **Customer Brand Interaction Approaches: Marketing Lever Evaluations**
  - ✓ Quantifies role of media and touch points in reaching customer with best message, time, and place
  - ✓ Supports allocation of resources to the various touch points to achieve planned exposure levels

---

The output of the analysis includes measures of the impact of various marketing plan elements, such as the elasticity of price, advertising, and promotion. These reveal the change in sales that is due to changes in the marketing variables based on historical data. For example, an increase of 100 GRPs for television advertising might yield a $100,000 increase in sales. It is most useful to interpret these measures when they have been converted to some kind of relative or normalized measure, such as elasticity, which reflects a percentage change in sales relative to the marketing input. Comparison across different inputs reveals the relative impact or "importance" of one marketing lever over another. When analyzed relative to the cost of investment, the different inputs translate into ROI measures. For example, the 100 GRPs have a dollar cost, which generates some amount of sales and profit. Firms can use incremental profit relative to investment cost to judge marketing effectiveness.

Ultimately, most marketers want to use modeling input to evaluate alternative marketing plan scenarios and to decide how to allocate future marketing investments. After a model has been established, the results can be housed in a decision-support system for running simulations, which often takes the form of replaying past history: "If we had spent 10% more on advertising, what sales increase might we have anticipated?" Ideally, simulations would be projected into future time periods: "What sales impact are we likely to see in the next planning period?" Model structure and business judgment will determine how prudent it is to use results in these ways.

The repeated application of simulation tools enables marketers to identify the best strategies to pursue. After taking into account modeled results, supply constraints, strategic goals, and other limitations, marketers can identify the optimal solution. Although it is possible to obtain a mathematical solution, this is often limited to one or a small number of variables, assuming that everything else is held constant. For example, marketers can conduct pricing optimization to achieve certain revenue goals if distribution and promotion are assumed to be constant. In practical terms, the best solution is often a combination of rigorous analysis and managerial assessments of the feasibility of execution.

Design

The sample comprises historical time periods during which the marketing elements and market response can be observed. It is desirable to have at least two years' worth of data to estimate the parameters of a time-series regression model with reasonable precision and to estimate seasonality, which is frequently an important driver of brand sales.

Ideally, the time periods are weekly, as many of the marketing inputs (e.g., GRPs for television advertising) change week to week and the consumer response to these is also observable week to week. Two years' worth of such measures provide 104 data points, which is sufficient for many applications. More data points, of course, are even better.

Key Data Inputs

Explicit measures must be collected for each marketing plan input and each time period. These become the independent variables for the model. Similarly, each sales response measure must be collected and aligned with time periods. Response measures can take on several forms (e.g., sales volume units, revenue dollars, profit dollars), which serve as the dependent variables in the model. It's best to have multiple measures to evaluate rather than to assume that one measure will always serve the purpose. The totality of all the measures effectively captures the marketing environment for the brand under study. Some formulations of mix modeling explicitly take into account the competitive environment. In this case, a parallel series of measures for each competitive brand must be collected.

An implication is that the model is estimated over a particular historical epoch and effectively represents that period. This means that the model analysis doesn't really provide evidence for situations that may occur in the future, when the firm implements more extreme values of the marketing plan. For example, if prices always range between $1.00 and $1.50, the model results can't be generalized (during the simulation phase) to prices that fall outside that range.

Firms can acquire data on marketing plan variables from any of the few syndicated data vendors, such as Nielsen Media Research. For brands that are not covered by syndicated services, another approach is necessary. Presumably, the advertiser knows what it is spending and may be able to capture that information through its advertising or media-buying agency or independently. The same issues hold for response data. Syndicated services such as Information Resources Inc. (widely known as IRI) provide sales data for many categories, especially in consumer packaged goods. Marketers will normally have a proprietary method of tracking their company's own sales but not those of their competitors.

The collection of data can become quite complex for companies that have multiple brands and stockkeeping units (SKUs), operate in multiple markets or regions, sell through multiple retail chains or dealers, and require periodic (e.g., annual) updating of analyses. The assembly and integration of data streams into a common data set for analysis can be a labor-intensive task that calls for its own solution.

Specialist companies have emerged recently to handle the data and automate the process as much as possible.

Illustrative Outputs

Typical outputs for marketing mix modeling show the estimated effects of each element of the mix on sales outcomes (Table 2.1 and Figure 2.8). Summarized over time, they show how the magnitudes of contributions have changed. The costs of alternative marketing investments are then integrated into the response analysis as part of the financial assessment of marketing (Figure 2.9). Simulation tools are used to systematically test alternative investment scenarios.

Implementation Issues

Gaining executive commitment. Marketing mix modeling can lead to improvements in marketing effectiveness that substantially exceed the costs of conducting analysis. (In other words, the application of mix modeling itself has a positive ROI.) However, mix modeling is relatively complex to understand and costly to execute, and it requires frequent updating as firms introduce new marketing plans and observe market responses. Given the considerable effort required to integrate mix modeling into a company's marketing operations, it's not surprising that marketers have not universally adopted it.

For modeling to be successful, the organization must have an understanding of how it will use modeling to maintain, stop, or modify certain types of marketing actions and allocate budget to different activities going forward. Equally as important, there must be a strong commitment from the executive team to take action on the results;

Table 2.1 ♦ Illustrative Output: Summarizing the Marketing Mix Effects

	2005			2006		
	Total	Off Season	In Season	Total	Off Season	In Season
Television	7%	9%	6%	13%	20%	4%
Print	5%	5%	5%	7%	12%	3%
Online	12%	18%	5%	7%	10%	3%

Figure 2.8 ◆ Illustrative Output: Decomposing the Marketing Mix Effects on Volume over Time

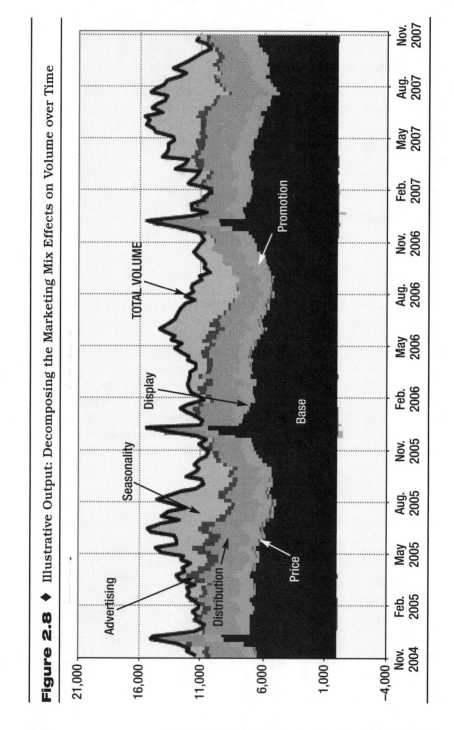

Figure 2.9 ♦ Illustrative Output: Assessing Financial Return

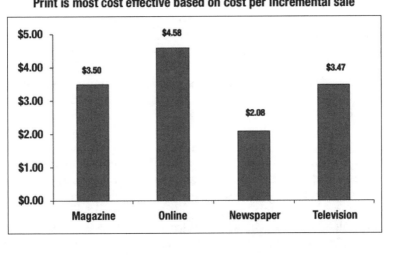

Print is most cost effective based on cost per incremental sale

without this commitment, the implementation can easily be derailed; even worse, a bad experience can make it difficult to reintroduce the approach for future cycles.

Gaining organizational commitment. Models are, of course, approximations of actual marketplace behavior. In general, they improve when more data are added and when they are more accurately specified to capture a more comprehensive set of marketplace patterns. This suggests a path to successful implementation that (1) begins with initial models that are constructed from readily available data (e.g., a subset of brands in the portfolio as compared with all brands) and (2) proceeds to more comprehensive and better models as firms apply knowledge gained from initial results and observe new response behavior and as more detailed data become relevant and available.

This approach builds organizational confidence incrementally as the methodological and business scope expands. An alternative is to seek a highly comprehensive and accurate model the first time around, which sets organizational expectations at a high level for definitive improvements in business performance. However, this can be excessively risky for companies just getting started with such a significant initiative.

Benefits and Limitations

A key benefit of mix modeling is the rigorous distillation and diagnosis of actual in-market performance for decision support. This method is strong on external validity; that is, it doesn't rely on self-reporting from consumers. Instead, it approximates the universe of the variables (e.g., all ad spend) and all sales in the market. The technique is comprehensive in its representation of all decision categories and variables in the marketing environment, whether controlled by marketers, competitors, or broader economic forces. It's not limited to a single marketing lever, such as advertising or promotion. Mix modeling also directly connects marketing decisions, customer behavioral response, and financial outcomes, all of which are critical elements that lead to successful ROI assessment.

Mix modeling heavily depends on large amounts of historical data, which means that it has limited application for untested marketing initiatives, such as new products, prices, or levels and types of media spend. Moreover, although mix modeling is popular in consumer packaged goods sectors in which third-party vendors make much of the needed data available, it is less applicable in other industries, such as financial services, telecommunications, and retail, in which raw data streams require high levels of customization to provide usable information for analysis.

In its basic form, mix modeling also doesn't address some potentially important marketing variables. For example, in general, firms ignore consumer segments when looking at overall markets. They also overlook intermediate stages of the marketing process, such as how advertising influences brand awareness, image, consideration, and preference, all of which may drive purchase behavior and have important implications for strategic marketing decisions. The long-term effects of marketing (which are often more significant than the short-term effects) are not well captured in mix models. Although extensions of mix modeling or other complementary methods can address these issues, it's fair to say that the basic model doesn't.

Bottom-Up Approaches: Customer Valuation

Customer valuation treats the customer as an asset. Firms can acquire, nurture, retain, and divest customers, as they can other assets. The basic axiom of this marketing discipline is to acknowledge that value is created when customers buy products and services and dissipates when they no longer buy. Therefore, the focus is on understanding customers' needs, behavior, and financial value and on planning the sequence of treatments they will receive over their lives as customers.

Marketing tasks in this approach include measuring current and future customer value by identifying all sources of revenue (e.g., product purchase, usage fees, service and repair) and aligning them with the costs associated with acquiring and managing customers on an ongoing basis (Figure 2.10). The business goal is to determine which customers to acquire, develop, and retain, according to their financial contribution to the firm. Analyses can determine the allowable amount of investment to manage individual customers (or groups), as well as the channels and vehicles to reach them and accomplish these goals.

Marketers ideally should be able to estimate the lifetime value of a customer (essentially the NPV of cash flows from the customer). Anticipated changes in this financial metric become the basis of marketing decisions about whether to make a particular offer to a customer, to attempt to cross-sell, or to save (i.e., retain) a customer who is likely to defect.

Design

The starting point for customer valuation is the population of current and potential customers. This approach builds up to the total market from all individual customers. The metrics are often quite different from those used in methods such as marketing mix modeling, which operates at the aggregate market level over time, with indicators such as aggregate sales or market share. Customer valu-

Figure 2.10 ♦ Understanding Customer Value: Decisions That Increase Portfolio Value

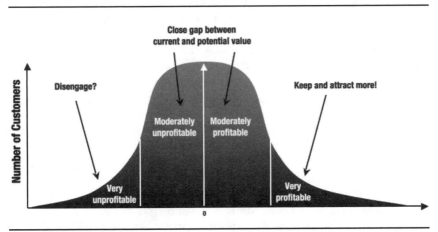

ation works with individual customers, so metrics might include the share of requirements for the customer, or share of wallet, in addition to valuation.

Another key feature of the design of a valuation approach is customer segmentation. Customers often are grouped into basic categories derived from usage characteristics. For example, credit card customers are grouped according to whether they always pay their charges by the due date or borrow money on their cards and pay it back over time; airline customers are grouped by frequency of flying; and telephone customers are grouped by rate plans.

Although the starting point is the customer, there is great emphasis on how they are treated through various marketing campaigns (e.g., direct-mail solicitations, frequent user program, customer care calls). Matching the ideal offer to the right customer is a key feature of a valuation approach to marketing resource allocation. Unlike mass marketing efforts, this approach uses information about the customer and seeks to benefit from improved responsiveness and greater value by tailoring offers fairly precisely.

Key Data Inputs

The essential requirements for customer valuation are revenue and costs associated with individual customers. For a retail bank, a customer may be anyone with a deposit, loan, or investment account. The relevant data to collect would include balances, payment, history, and contacts with the bank through such channels as branches, call centers, or online. Marketing investment inputs are characterized by campaigns or specific communications to individual customers and their responses to them.

Cost data would include acquisition channel and cost to serve the customer (e.g., time spent using resources such as call centers or branch tellers). The estimation of costs by customer or customer type is often a difficult measurement task. Many of the costs are fixed, as they come from prior investments in infrastructure such as the branch, telephone call center, and the people who staff them.

Marketing plan data come in the form of specific campaigns, their target customers, dates, and timing and customer response profiles. Ideally, the same individual customer can be linked between one campaign and another. This is critical for firms to be able to measure (as closely as possible) the customer's entire experience with the provider, not simply his or her response to a single marketing stimulus.

For example, there is growing evidence that the deeper the customer relationship is (as measured by multiple product and service purchases), the greater is the customer value. Firms need a complete profile of customer information to test the accuracy of this proposition and to take action on it in subsequent offers.

Illustrative Outputs

An important output to examine is the distribution of customer value (Figure 2.10). The typical pattern shows a small percentage of valuable customers that account for a disproportionate amount of profit (Figure 2.11). In the airline industry, for example, it is not unusual to observe that 5% of customers account for 95% of profit. The actual size breakdown into groups of "somewhat profitable," "break-even," and "unprofitable" customers has direct strategic implications. The typical challenges for marketers are the following:

♦ To retain the most profitable customers without increasing spending to the point of diminishing profitability;

♦ To change the behavior of unprofitable or marginally profitable customers to improve profitability through pricing, product offers, or service support; and

♦ To develop new target customers who appear similar in profile or response behavior to current profitable customers.

Firms can induce behavior change through experimental testing on a sample of customers and systematically varying and market testing elements such as price, delivery, messaging, and features. From actual customer response behavior, firms can develop a predictive model to calibrate the elasticity of each dimension, which leads to the optimization of responses across all dimensions.

Figure 2.11 ♦ Illustrative Output: Distribution of Lifetime Value of Customer Is Heavily Concentrated

---

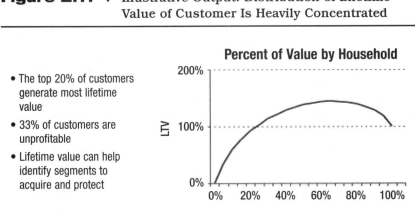

- The top 20% of customers generate most lifetime value
- 33% of customers are unprofitable
- Lifetime value can help identify segments to acquire and protect

---

Predictive models are also used with existing profile data to find prospects who match the ideal, most profitable customers. These propensity models can be built with logistic regression or interaction-based models, such as chi-square automatic interaction detector (known as CHAID) or classification and regression trees (CART) to allow for more flexibility in the functional form of models.

Implementation Issues

Customer valuation methods are the backbone of many customer relationship management (CRM) systems. Some of the most common implementation issues arise from the larger CRM system, of which valuation is a part. Many companies have made significant investments in information technology to power their CRM systems, which they consider central to capturing the customer-level information needed to tailor marketing stimuli to targeted customers and segments. Large data warehouses are built to house virtually every customer transaction, across all channels and other touch points with customers. Tracking systems and software are necessary to extract value from the data for marketing purposes.

On occasion, the scope of technology emphasis can obscure the original aim of CRM: to build customer value through appropriate acquisition, development, and retention activities. If technology trumps business issues, there is great risk of failure. Indeed, many companies have concluded that CRM has failed and that high information technology costs are a major reason. In contrast, if business issues drive technology deployment, there is a greater likelihood that the technology will be built to the level needed rather than to the level that is possible. With this approach, the CRM system can demonstrate its value incrementally, thus improving its chances for overall success.

Silo Mentality

Customer value measures aggregate revenues and costs from different parts of the organization. For example, bank revenues can come from demand deposit accounts, investment accounts, loans of various types, and services such as asset management. Most organizations have historically treated such specific products as separate business units up to a certain point. Often, no one department focuses on the entire customer experience. Employee incentives are designed to encourage product sales rather than to improve total customer value; however, this makes for conflict when firms measure and act on customer level profitability.

There are exceptions. Some firms have enterprise customer or total customer experience management programs and teams assigned to develop the broad customer relationship. These teams must compel individual business units to collaborate and act with broader corporate goals in mind, not just those of their individual units.

Need for New Organizational Processes

As a consequence of the silo mentality, there is often a need to build new customer-oriented marketing processes, such as for customer analysis, offer design, and in-market execution. Without new processes, the best data, tools, infrastructure, and analysts won't create financial value. This approach often requires significant internal and external resources and several years to accomplish. As such, some companies choose to start small, and they look to a business unit or some other part of the company to formally break the existing processes in the spirit of work-arounds that allow them to demonstrate the ideal benefits of CRM and valuation. Companies can then scale up this pilot approach to more business units and eventually to the whole company.

Benefits and Limitations

The use of customer valuation to make marketing resource decisions can improve business performance by matching the value of the customer to the company with the value that the company brings to the customer. Rather than offer to serve any customer who appears, customer valuation encourages optimal selectivity, in that companies will select and treat customers only to the extent that they generate a reasonable return for the company. The best (current and potential) customers will receive an investment on behalf of the company that is commensurate with their high value. The low-value and unprofitable customers will receive only that amount of investment that sustains profitability or changes them to profitable levels. For example, companies can offer low-value customers e-mail help lines for service or opportunities to pay incrementally for a service representative rather than a live service representative.

When properly applied, customer value methods enable a company's marketers to use marketing funds efficiently. For example, a direct marketer of books and music discovered that a significant segment of its customers never (over a five-year span) purchased its products even though they had responded to trial offers. Identifying these customer types enabled the company to cease mailings to them, which potentially saved dramatically on mailing costs.

Valuation is usually an inward-focused method; in other words, it estimates the value of a customer only from experiences with the company itself. Such a method can, unfortunately, prevent the company from seeing the potential value of either customers who currently favor competitors or prospective customers who have not yet entered the category. For this reason, companies may choose to supplement valuation methods with other techniques to get at potential value that measures things that are external to the company, such as discrete choice experiments with new products or features, competitive brand performance to identify underserved customers, or share-of-wallet surveys to quantify the total amount of business customers that might be available.

Similarly, the valuation method has the potential to be overly backward focused because it draws all its information from the past history of customer transactions. It's important to anticipate where customer needs will evolve to in the future, but customer valuation methods don't offer much insight there. Lifetime value calculations are predicated on projections of future cash flows, so they have a forward direction. However, such forecasts are typically based on historical data at the individual customer level, and thus they can't reflect all possible future dynamics of customer demand.

Customer Brand Interaction Approaches: Marketing Lever Evaluations

An emerging set of methods focuses on the connection between consumers and marketing touch points, which include advertising media, promotion, distribution channels, retail experience, usage experience, buzz, product placement, and many other brand stimuli. Typically, such methods seek to understand the role of multiple media and touch points in reaching the customer with the right message at the right time and place (not necessarily generating the specific response) to better allocate resources to the various touch points. These techniques are becoming more relevant because of the proliferation of new media channels, especially those that consumers initiate, such as blogs and opinions expressed on cogenerated sites.

Design

Several of the designs for touch-point measurement are based on surveys. If the goal of the method is to measure the influence of the full range of connection points, or at least a large portion of them, then surveys are a must. There is no existing, passive source for all touch points, and self-reporting provides marketing analysts with a window on the most at one time within the same measurement system.

Self-reports can be retrospective, as when consumers report on all the touch points they normally experience or have experienced within some defined period, such as the previous month. A variation on this approach is experience sampling or occasion-based sampling, in which specific instances of interaction of the consumer and the marketing environment are selected according to some type of probabilistic selection. For example, a wireless electronic device might prompt a consumer at random time points to report on what he or she sees, hears, and feels in that moment. Respondents could also be sampled on different days of the week and asked to report on what they saw, heard, and consumed, such as a sample of all occasions in the past 24 hours.

Sample sizes need to be large enough to capture the full range of consumer segments. For low-incidence touch points, such as service interactions or Internet communications (based on the population at large), this creates significant challenges.

Key Data Inputs

Questions of brand–consumer interaction can cover topics such as attitudes and perceptions of the particular interaction points, the extent to which those interaction points form specific brand images, and purchase or usage measures associated with those instances. When constructing surveys, researchers must consider respondents' questionnaire burden. When the number of touch points is high (they can easily run to 30 or more), the burden multiplies for each questionnaire item. An important criterion for selecting items is the extent to which an item differentiates the touch points' influence on consumer brand metrics.

Illustrative Outputs

The basic measures reflect the power of alternative touch points to influence consumers and support budget allocation decisions. Measures of the conversion of consumer intent to purchase indicate the relative impact of prior demand compared with point-of-sale levers and support mix decisions at both points in the purchase process (Figure 2.12).

Implementation Issues

Measuring the impact of multiple consumer touch points is a new type of marketing and communications research that cuts across traditional advertising messages, media selection, and overall brand management. A challenge for firms is to tailor the method to the needs of the different constituents, each of which has unique standards for sound research. For example, media specialists have strong views on the measurement of audience sizes, reach, frequency, and opportunity to see a stimulus. Those responsible for advertising are especially

Figure 2.12 ♦ Drivers of Preference and Sales Activation

Different touch points build brand preference and create impact at the point of sale.

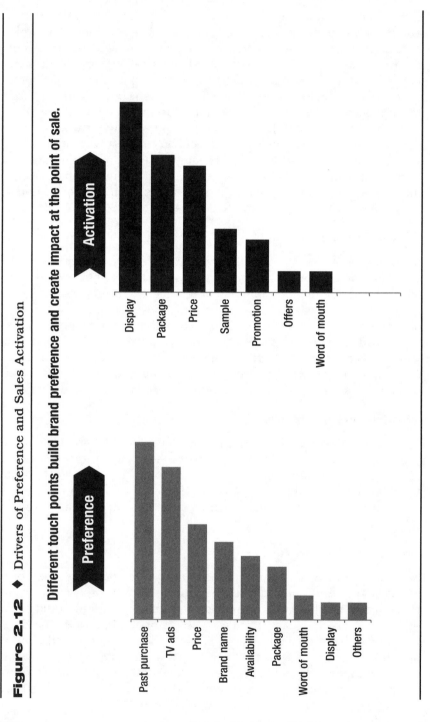

interested in the content of the message and how well it conveys the intended strategy. Brand managers are interested in all these topics, but they clearly have great interest in budget setting and allocation decisions that cut across traditional categories such as specific media.

There are some signs of an emerging discipline of experience planning, which is analogous to media planning for paid media. As companies become more interested in managing the full range of touch points, including some they don't totally control, such as external blogs, there will likely be more of an established organization, team, or agency to focus on this.

Benefits and Limitations

Evaluating marketing levers can provide a holistic view of all consumer interactions with the brand, which enables rational, efficient, and effective decision making about resource deployment. Partisans of the top-down or bottom-up methods may argue for the more established, rigorous, hard data (i.e., not self-report data) approaches. However, it's difficult to stand on methods that are, by definition, incomplete in their outlook and to avoid softer methods simply because measurement and analytical precision hasn't arrived yet. The difficulty of measurement doesn't justify ignoring it. To do so can lead to biased analyses and conclusions.

For example, customer experiences with a brand through service encounters influence their future intentions to stay with the brand or switch. What's the right combination of actual operational service changes versus communications changes to address a customer defection problem? A strictly market-level communication approach (supported by mix modeling) probably isn't adequate. Fixing the underlying problem may not accomplish its goals if it's not properly communicated.

These methods have the potential to fill an important gap between the top-down and bottom-up approaches. They are limited by dependence on consumer retrospective reporting and the fact that they do not necessarily get at the ultimate financially based outcome measures. They may quantify the financial impact in the sense of cost to reach the target audience, but they may not give direct evidence that the stimulus leads to increased sales response.

◆ CONCLUSIONS, IMPLICATIONS, AND RECOMMENDATIONS

There are many challenges for firms to achieve a disciplined approach to the measurement and management of marketing effectiveness. Can firms make marketing resource allocation decisions without systematically going through all these issues and questions? Yes, and they are made all the time, without the benefit of considering all these elements. The extent of planned approaches to resource allocation is quite uneven across industries and types and sizes of companies.

As accountability has become an imperative, marketers are being pressed to apply as much rigor as is feasible to the decisions they make. What this translates into in practice depends on the nature of the market being served, as well as on the company and its resources. I offer up this review of the methods used in marketing today in the spirit of examples, and I make no claim of being exhaustive (though I have included the major applications to my knowledge). In conclusion, I summarize several themes that emerged and offer some judgments on their implications for practice.

No Single Tool

There is a plethora of tools, techniques, technologies, methods, and approaches that can be applied to gain control over and improve marketing investments. However, there is no single tool that can comprehensively deal with all the issues at once. For example, although marketing mix modeling is important to quantify the contributions of advertising and promotion spending, price, and distribution at the market level, over time, it typically doesn't help with assessment of the impact of marketing expenditures targeted at specific segments, user groups, or prior responders to marketing. Customer valuation methods address the individual customer–level response issues but provide no input on aggregate market impact. Top-down approaches are likely a good choice for big ad spenders. Bottom-up methods are especially apt for direct marketers. Customer-brand interactive techniques are important for those companies that rely on Internet channels.

More Organizational Than Analytical Work

There is as much or more work to be done in orchestrating the processes of investment management in the organization as there is in carrying out analytical work. An analytically "correct" answer (e.g., optimize spending by increasing it by X percentage) isn't going to achieve optimal response unless it is correctly implemented in the organization and in the market.

Firms often impose strategic constraints on budget allocations that depart from pure optimization of profit. For example, a global computer firm allocated a certain number of SKUs to each of its major regions (North and South America, Europe, Asia, and Africa) to tailor products to local needs. A pure profit maximization strategy would have allocated virtually all SKUs to the current largest markets (the Americas and Europe).

Organizational activities (align, adopt, and adapt) often involve more people and more interactions among players than do analytical activities:

♦ Alignment involves leadership and project teams.

♦ Adoption involves operations and agencies.

♦ Adaptation involves communication with all the preceding groups.

♦ Analysis involves mainly analysts.

Continuous Improvement

There are several reasons companies would want to adopt a continuous improvement perspective rather than an aspiration to get it right the first time. It takes time to build capabilities, and companies learn what they need and can use by using it. Data availability is a constraint and sometimes a barrier to progress, but time and resources can overcome such constraints.

The improved measurement and management of marketing effectiveness doesn't necessarily require significant out-of-pocket expense to execute; it can be done on a budget. Companies should apply solutions that require significant infrastructure investment (e.g., CRM software) cautiously and with a dose of ROI thinking.

Change is the normal course of business (e.g., monthly profits and losses lead to tactical change; quarterly reports lead to budget revision). Marketing processes normally change, too. Most investments don't involve grand strategy or regime changes; they are based on incremental decisions and periodic adjustments.

How can firms acquire the skills and capabilities to implement this type of process? There are, of course, formal educational programs in management and organizational development that should be considered. From a practice perspective, there are professional organizations (the American Marketing Association, the Advertising Research Foundation, and the Marketing Science Institute) that, in their own unique formats, facilitate information sharing through conferences, publications, and workshops. There is more to be done to stimulate networking among companies that are just starting to build capabilities, to assist them through the difficult task of introducing new approaches into a traditional environment.

Other important sources to tap for knowledge about the links between marketing and financial performance are published articles and books. The references identified at the end of this chapter are useful for their broad coverage of the issues, examples of applications, and references to more sources for further exploration.

Marketing and Finance

Marketing measurement and management is about joining marketing and financial disciplines; without proper integration of the two perspectives, the exercise is less likely to succeed. Granted, some elements of these two disciplines are separate, distinct, and possibly even conflicting. Marketing people are often creative, intuitive, and open to possibilities, whereas finance people are typically "left brain," data driven, and eager to close problems.

Still, there should be common interests around topics such as innovation. Many companies expect marketing to be the source of innovation and growth, which is needed for financial health. Numerous marketing effectiveness and brand value research initiatives show that marketing assets demonstrate financial value, and marketing and finance must continue to work together to demonstrate this financial value.

Finally, the task of creating a disciplined approach to marketing effectiveness and resource expenditure may seem daunting, especially for smaller companies. However, such companies can make progress even on a small budget, as they have already made much of the required resource commitment in fixed costs for people and infrastructure. As the thinking and activities become part of everyday practice, and not a special project, the approach and the process should become easier to maintain.

◆ FURTHER READINGS

Almquist, Eric and Gordon Wyner (2001), "Boost Your Marketing ROI with Experimental Design," *Harvard Business Review,* 79 (October), 135–41.

CMO Council (2008), "Marketing Outlook 2008: Executive Summary," (accessed February 28, 2008), [available athttp://www.cmocouncil.org/resources/form_mo_execsummary.asp].

Gupta, Sunil and Donald R. Lehmann (2005), *Managing Customers as Investment: The Strategic Value of Customers in the Long Run.* Upper Saddle River, NJ: Wharton School Publishing.

Keller, Kevin Lane and Donald R. Lehmann (2006) "Brands and Branding: Research Findings and Future Priorities," *Marketing Science,* 25 (6), 740–55.

Lehmann, Donald R. and David Reibstein (2006), *Marketing Metrics and Financial Performance.* Cambridge, MA: Marketing Science Institute.

CHAPTER 3

PRACTICAL MEASUREMENT OF ADVERTISING IMPACT: THE IBM EXPERIENCE

Todd M. Powers, IBM
Anil Menon, IBM

◆ INTRODUCTION

As a major international supplier of information technology (IT) products and services, including computer hardware, software, and services, as well as business consulting services, IBM Corporation invests hundreds of millions of dollars annually in marketing communications. The Market Intelligence team that supports the Integrated Marketing Communications (IMC) organization at IBM is committed to providing feedback about the performance of those communications in the marketplace to ensure that the investments bear fruit.

The IMC organization covers all the different vehicles through which IBM communicates with its audiences of interest. We have teams that focus on the separate functions in IMC, including advertising, demand generation, events, and sponsorships. In turn, each of these functions uses research to maximize the effectiveness of those efforts. For example, for years, IBM has been a sponsor of the U.S. Open tennis tournament in Flushing Meadows, N.Y., hosted by the U.S. Tennis Association. IBM builds and maintains the U.S. Open Web site, where upward of 6 million tennis fans come for facts, figures, and tournament updates for this great sporting event. An IBM-pioneered feature that drew interest in 2006 was called "PointTracker," an online visual display that enabled viewers to follow the path of the ball as two contestants played out a point (Figure 3.1).

Well, IBM wanted to know whether this sponsorship is paying dividends. As such, Market Intelligence (MI) has conducted online surveys with visitors to the site, asking about their experience and gauging the impact of the experience on their perceptions of IBM. Questions cover viewers' interests in tennis and in the tournament itself, about how and how often they use the Web site, about awareness of IBM's sponsorship of the site, and about their image of IBM and their openness to doing business with IBM.

The results of this research inform the sponsorship marketing team at IBM about the relative value of association with this sporting event. Are IT decision makers who visit the U.S. Open Web site aware that IBM designed and developed the site? If so, do they hold a more positive opinion of IBM than of its counterparts? Are they more interested in engaging IBM? Over time, survey feedback has enabled IBM to improve the Web site and to help justify the overall investment.

Similar research efforts are undertaken routinely to test other marketing communications efforts. In this chapter, we focus on one area in particular: advertising. We believe that our systematic approach to advertising research at IBM is unique among business-to-business advertisers.

♦ ADVERTISING RESEARCH APPROACH

IBM uses primary research to test its advertising at key stages during the ad development process. Throughout this process, the MI team works closely with its IMC colleagues at IBM and partners at Ogilvy & Mather, IBM's advertising agency of record. The expectation is that IBM researchers will learn things at all stages and use the insights gained to drive consistent improvements in the company's advertising work.

Figure 3.2 provides a generalized model of the advertising implementation process at IBM. The rationale for an advertising campaign (or for an individual execution, for that matter) typically emerges from the current business strategy at the corporation. An ad brief is developed for the agency, laying out all the objectives the advertising is intended to meet. From this a plan is built. Creative types at the agency develop the images and messaging that will comprise the advertising, and early versions of the ads are produced. At this time, media plans are also crafted. Following various internal reviews and

Figure 3.1 ◆ PointTracker Visual Display

Figure 3.2 ◆ Generalized Model of IBM Advertising Implementation

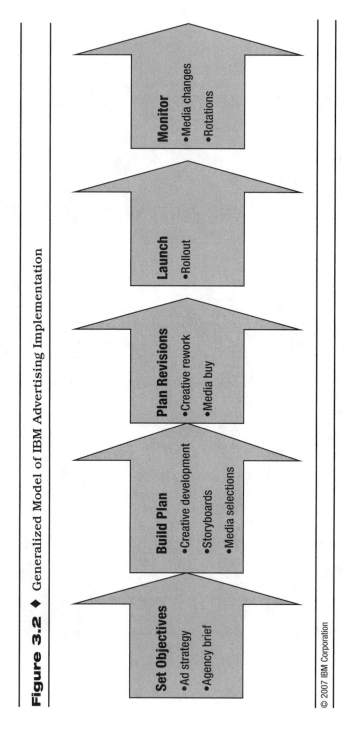

Set Objectives
•Ad strategy
•Agency brief

Build Plan
•Creative development
•Storyboards
•Media selections

Plan Revisions
•Creative rework
•Media buy

Launch
•Rollout

Monitor
•Media changes
•Rotations

any external testing, plan revisions are made, and a media buy is executed. The campaign is then launched, and monitoring activities are implemented to provide ongoing management of the investment.

Throughout this process, we use research to help guide development of the advertising. Figure 3.3 shows the three basic research methods that are typically deployed, and these are designed to provide input at different stages of the process.

Qualitative Research

Early in advertising development, IBM is likely to use exploratory, qualitative research—in general, focus groups or individual interviews (IDIs)—to provide feedback on the advertising, particularly if it is embarking on a completely new campaign. Qualitative research methods are flexible and a relatively inexpensive means of understanding whether the advertising is on track.

As a rule, we want to accomplish at least three objectives with the qualitative research. First, we want to know whether the advertising truly communicates the intended messages. As we noted previously, we will have a fully specified ad brief developed at this point, and we want to know whether the advertising completely and accurately delivers on the objectives of the brief. For example, if an objective of the advertising is to reinforce the belief, among our line-of-business decision-maker audience, that IBM is a premier provider of business consulting services, we would look for evidence that focus-group participants readily reflect this notion on exposure to the early ad executions. Different techniques or exercises might be used to investigate message communication, but the general assessment at the conclusion of the research is an answer to the question, "Did they get it?"

A second key objective of the qualitative research is to understand whether the message that has been communicated is of value. Do the research participants react positively to the advertising concept? Here, we look not so much to provide specific feedback about individual ads we may be testing; rather, we hope to gain insights into the overall appropriateness of the approach, or theme, of the advertising. Again, multiple techniques might be used to investigate these issues. Often, projective qualitative techniques, such as laddering or sentence-completion exercises, yield rich insights into the impact of the advertising on our audiences.

A third objective of our qualitative research is to determine whether there are any unintended negative consequences that result from exposure to the ads or ad concepts. Occasionally, we find that proposed advertising communicates something that we simply had not antici-

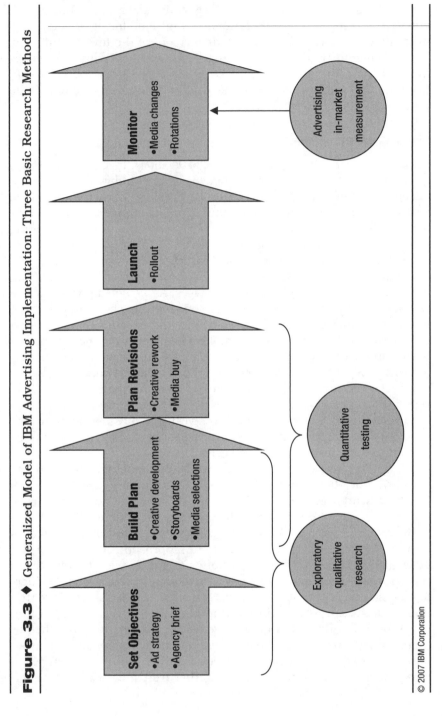

Figure 3.3 ◆ Generalized Model of IBM Advertising Implementation: Three Basic Research Methods

Set Objectives
•Ad strategy
•Agency brief

Build Plan
•Creative development
•Storyboards
•Media selections

Plan Revisions
•Creative rework
•Media buy

Launch
•Rollout

Monitor
•Media changes
•Rotations

Exploratory qualitative research

Quantitative testing

Advertising in-market measurement

pated and that would be deleterious to our overall image among the target audience. In these cases, we can often make relatively simple changes to the ads to remove the problematic interpretation.

It is important to note that, by its very nature, qualitative research provides only general feedback about the likely impact of advertising. It is not possible to project findings from this research to a larger population with any degree of confidence. As such, we do not look to draw a representative sample of target respondents for our focus groups or IDIs. Instead, we want to find as many different perspectives as we expect to encounter across the audience. Thus, we might recruit participants from different geographies, industries, job functions, and so forth, to round out our respondent population. In some cases, we bring people with considerably different perspectives into a single focus-group discussion and observe the interplay as the discussion unfolds. At other times, we assemble more homogeneous individual groups, but we purposefully juxtapose the groups to allow for comparisons. On completion of our qualitative research, we want to be comfortable that we gave our target audience every opportunity to provide constructive criticism.

Quantitative Testing

Figure 3.3 shows that a secondary phase of research in the advertising development process at IBM is typically some form of quantitative testing. The two key methods we deploy during this stage are copy testing and controlled experimentation. Both research techniques are intended to provide feedback that can be projected (within the limits of statistical precision) to the intended audience of the advertising.

There are many highly qualified firms that provide copy-testing services to advertisers that want to ensure, as best possible, the optimization of their advertising investments. In recent years, IBM has partnered with Ameritest, of Albuquerque, N.Mex., for copy-testing services. Our approach with Ameritest in copy testing is to pit our proposed advertising against norms we have developed over time to ensure that only the executions that meet or exceed threshold values eventually make it to the marketplace.

Research respondents are recruited to central facilities in countries where we plan for our advertising to run. There they are exposed to ads from IBM and its competitors and asked a battery of questions. Some of this feedback is a reliable gauge of the likely performance of the advertisement in question after it is placed into rotation. Other feedback provides diagnostic interpretations of the specific strengths and weaknesses of the ads.

Two key copy-testing metrics we use to evaluate newly developed ads are "branded attention" and "motivation." Branded attention is the combination of attention and brand linkage. It reflects the percentage of people who selected the test ad as "interesting" and who mentioned IBM as the sponsor. Motivation is the percentage of respondents who, after reexposure to the test ad, said that the ad increased their interest considerably or somewhat (see Figure 3.4) in doing business with the sponsor of the ad (on a five-point scale).

Figure 3.4 shows the results of a 2007 test of an IBM television ad developed for the Systems and Technology Group (STG). In the figure, the test ad is plotted against the 50 most recently tested STG ads that received at least 150 gross rating points (GRPs) when placed into rotation in the United States. Clearly, the ad performed well, and as a result, it was deemed to be a viable candidate for eventual rollout.

In addition to the overall performance measures cited previously, copy testing also provides numerous metrics designed to give diagnostic insights about aspects of the ads that might benefit from alterations. A good example for television advertising is Ameritest's Flow of Emotion analysis. In this procedure, research respondents who have viewed a television ad as part of copy-testing research are shown individual images (15 to 20 snapshots drawn from different points in the ad film) in random order and then are asked to rate each image (on a positive to negative scale). The results are summarized across all respondents, and the output is plotted in a line graph superimposed with selected images from the ad. Figure 3.5 shows an example from the IBM television ad "Love Is in the Air," which aired in 2002.

In Figure 3.5, "Picture Number" refers to the images from the ad, listed in the order in which they appeared. The solid line shows the percentage of research participants who scored each image highly positively, and the dashed line shows the percentage who rated the images very negatively. The dotted lines are norms for positive and negative ratings, developed over time.

The Flow of Emotion for "Love Is in the Air" follows the emotional build structure, with a rise in positive emotion peaking on the reveal of the IBM brand. Key images that provide positive emotional response are depicted at various peaks in Figure 3.5. The positive emotion builds over the course of the ad, and the ad finishes with a strong emotional connection to the IBM brand identification. This ad also has no strong negative emotions that might need to be revised.

Ameritest also provides a similar diagnostic metric, the Flow of Attention graphic, which helps researchers understand which images in an ad capture the attention of the viewer. These measures, used in combination with feedback on issues such as liking, strategic communica-

Figure 3.4 ◆ Test of 2007 STG Ad

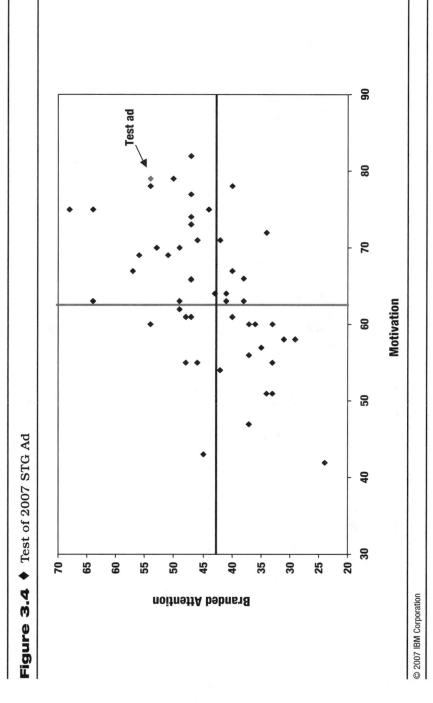

Figure 3.5 ◆ Flow of Emotion Analysis for "Love Is in the Air"

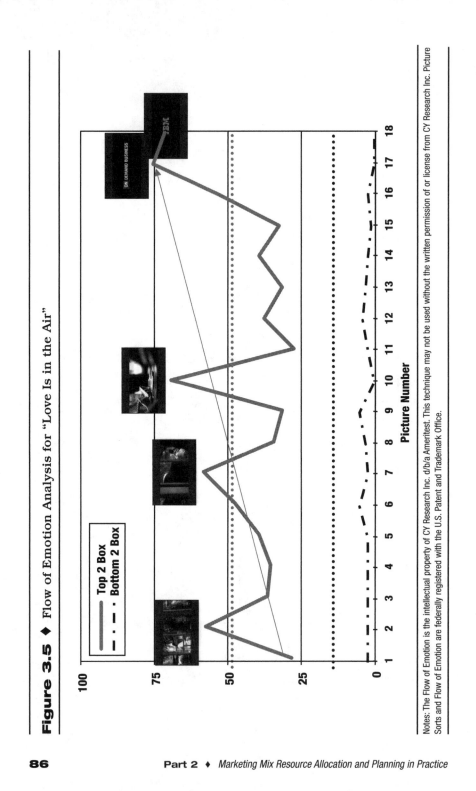

tion, relevance, and calls-to-action, provide considerable detail about how various audiences are likely to respond to any given advertisement. (For a complete description of copy-testing theory and practice as developed by Ameritest, see *The Advertising Research Handbook*, by Charles E. Young.)

Another quantitative technique used effectively at IBM to understand the factors that influence advertising performance is controlled experiments. Experimental designs enable us to manipulate advertising-related variables selectively and to measure the responses. This can be done in a test or simulated environment, or in actual market conditions. A recent example from work conducted in the United States illustrates the benefits of this approach.

In 2005, IBM was looking to increase its penetration among one segment of its customers and prospects. We had developed a series of new products and services to meet the needs of these companies, and we were preparing to go to market with the offerings. The IMC organization was charged with creating an advertising and communications strategy to support the rollout. The team was confident that it had found an effective creative message to promote the new offerings, but it was unsure about the level of investment required and had questions about the most appropriate media for the advertising.

Market Intelligence designed an in-market test in the United States, which systematically manipulated the variables and used a combination of survey- and business-based metrics to evaluate the outcome. Figure 3.6 depicts the overall design, a pretest/posttest control group methodology.

As Figure 3.6 shows, the test design included six cells. Two cities were placed in each cell to minimize the potential negative consequences of an unanticipated problem, such as a natural catastrophe or an economic anomaly. Cities were selected on the basis of demographic, economic, and business indicators, and they were randomly assigned to test conditions. Participating firms were headquarters or single-site companies located in 12 metropolitan statistical areas, including Charlotte, N.C.; Cleveland; Pittsburgh; St. Louis; Orlando, Fla.; Nashville; Portland, Ore.; Denver; Indianapolis; Hartford, Conn.; Raleigh, N.C.; and Columbus, Ohio.

We completed two telephone surveys in each city, one as a pretest and the other approximately eight months after the advertising plans had been in market. The surveys measured perceptions and behaviors toward IBM and its competitors, as well as specific feedback on the advertising and communications efforts. We also collected nonsurvey business metrics (e.g., pipeline, revenues, calls to a toll-free number), again in pre- and posttest time frames.

Figure 3.6 ♦ Design of In-Market Test

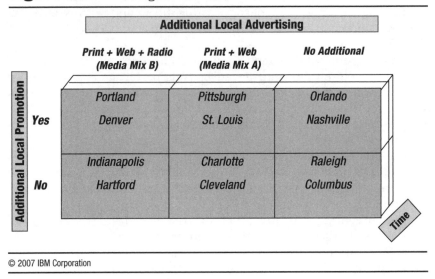

© 2007 IBM Corporation

The key variables manipulated in the test were the local advertising plan and the local promotion plan. The advertising plans reflected three distinct levels, as the columns of Figure 3.6 show. Two cells received no additional advertising (beyond the normal, day-to-day efforts already in place). Two cells received additional advertising that comprised print and online ads, and the remaining two cells also received additional advertising, but the media mix included print, Web, and radio advertising. Local promotions (most notably events and direct mail) were either present or absent, as the rows of Figure 3.6 show.

There were many insights from this experiment, and we note several here. First, we found evidence that the advertising was, indeed, having some of its intended effects. Figure 3.7 shows pre- and posttest measures from the survey results that pertain to respondents' openness to doing business with IBM. For both "Likelihood to seek out information about IBM" and "Likelihood to recommend IBM," we saw modest increases in the posttest. When we looked at the responses of those who recognized the advertising and attributed it to IBM, we saw that such decision makers showed higher levels of awareness, consideration, and preference for IBM than decision makers who did not recognize the advertising.

We also found differences in survey metrics by experimental cell. In particular, media mix B (print, Web, and radio) + local promotions (events and direct mail), the condition executed in Portland and

Figure 3.7 ♦ Pre- and Posttest Measures on Openness to Doing Business with IBM

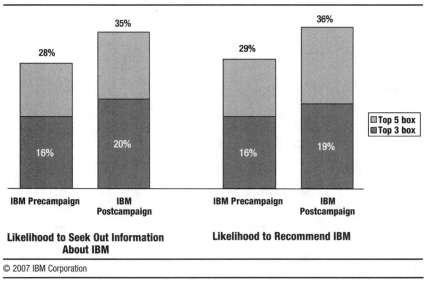

IBM Precampaign | IBM Postcampaign | IBM Precampaign | IBM Postcampaign

Likelihood to Seek Out Information About IBM

Likelihood to Recommend IBM

Top 5 box
Top 3 box

© 2007 IBM Corporation

Denver, had strong scores for awareness of the advertising, familiarity with the program of offerings, interest in contact from IBM, and preference for IBM as a supplier of products and services.

Among the business metrics, we also saw many differences. Of special interest, of course, is revenues. As Figure 3.8 shows, IBM revenues with target companies in the test markets increased most markedly with the addition of local advertising, especially for media mix B. Local promotions had limited effects, with the possible exception of the condition without any additional advertising.

In-Market Measurement

Since early 2002, IBM has monitored its investment in advertising using a tracking survey called Advertising In-Market Measurement (AIM). Using a hybrid telephone and Internet research instrument, we survey each year upward of 6500 qualified company decision makers in 12 countries about their perceptions of IBM and its competitors and about their interactions with relevant advertising.

This comprehensive set of surveys—we have different AIM executions for the different advertising target audiences—has provided

Figure 3.8 ♦ Revenue Change in Test Markets

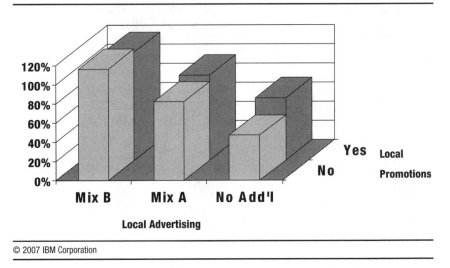

© 2007 IBM Corporation

immediate feedback about the performance of our ad campaigns in the market, and it has been a key influence on the general direction of our ongoing advertising strategy.

Sampled companies are contacted by telephone, and qualified respondents are identified through a series of screening questions. The interview proper takes approximately 25 to 30 minutes to complete, depending in part on the detail the respondent provides. Initially, we inquire about advertising that they may have encountered recently and record unaided recall for ads on television, in print (newspaper or magazine), or on the Internet. The next series of questions covers brand consideration and preference for IBM and up to four competitors. A third set covers favorable selling environment (FSE), a module that we explain in some detail in a later section. Subsequent segments of the questionnaire cover brand image attributes, recent brand purchases, and demographics.

At this point in the interview process, respondents are asked to point their Web browsers to a designated URL. Once there, survey participants are shown image collages drawn from television, print, and/or Internet advertising. The images have been debranded, which means that all logos and other brand-identifying marks have been edited out. After they view each collage, respondents indicate whether they recognize the images and, if so, whether they can identify the sponsor of the ad(s). (In the relatively rare instances in which participants do not have access to the Internet, interviewers read verbal descriptions of the ads.)

The online portion of the AIM surveys described in the preceding paragraphs has been pivotal in helping us gauge the impact of our advertising in-market. Recognition is a superior measure to the more typical open-recall question as an indicator of exposure to advertising. Using responses to the collage recognition questions, we can classify our respondents into "exposed" and "unexposed" groups. People who recognize a collage are classified as "exposed," regardless of whether they can later correctly identify the sponsor of the advertising. Thus, we can compare the responses of these two groups of respondents to other survey questions and attribute any meaningful differences to their exposure to the advertising.

We should note here that a criticism of this exposed versus unexposed comparison methodology is the well-documented fact that a company's existing customers are more likely to attend to its advertising. In general, the reasoning is that IBM customers who might otherwise simply flip past an ad in a magazine see an IBM logo and stop, thinking, "I buy products from this company. Let's see what they are promoting these days." This tendency makes customers more likely to fall into the exposed group, which in turn leads the exposed group to be more positive about IBM. For this reason, we always look at our results two ways: first overall and second within customer sets. Are customers who have been exposed to our ads more positive about IBM than customers who have not been exposed? Does that hold true for noncustomers, as well? Although these safeguards are not foolproof, we believe that they help ensure that we get a clear picture of our advertising.

The measurements in our AIM surveys are intended to provide feedback about performance at various stages of the classical marketing funnel. Figure 3.9 shows a typical marketing funnel and the associated AIM measures. Near the top of the funnel are measures of awareness and recognition, as we discussed previously. Lower down the funnel are brand-image metrics. Given the need to cover many other advertising-related topics in our AIM surveys, we can afford only limited space for image questions. We currently have a battery of six questions that cover characteristics such as leadership and innovation that we ask our survey participants. These questions are asked about IBM and about each competitor covered in the survey.

The next set of questions reflected in our funnel of Figure 3.9 addresses consideration and preference. We want to know (again, for IBM and for each competitor) how willing the decision makers are to consider a company when they buy relevant products and services. We also want to know which company is their preferred vendor.

The final set of metrics is contained in our FSE module, described briefly previously. With these questions, we measure how open our

Figure 3.9 ♦ Measurement of the Marketing Funnel Stages in AIM

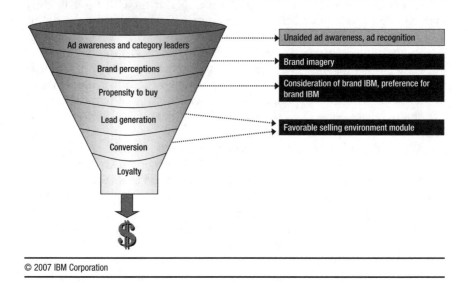

target companies are to doing business with IBM and others. There are six items that constitute the FSE module, and we track each separately, along with an openness composite score derived from the six. For each competitor, respondents indicate how likely they are to

♦ Recommend [company] to a colleague,

♦ Seek out more information about [company]'s products and services (e.g., visit the company's Web site, visit its booth at conferences or trade shows, call the company, request product or service information, or click on an online ad),

♦ Meet or take a call with [company]'s sales representatives,

♦ Identify yourself to [company] as being interested in its products or services,

♦ Ask colleagues about their opinions or experiences with [company], and

♦ Request a bid or proposal from [company].

All the AIM survey measures discussed herein are used to assess the impact of IBM's advertising in the marketplace. Performance on such measures guides decisions about continued use of the current advertising, as well as campaigns that may be planned for the future. For example, consider Table 3.1, which shows first-quarter recognition

Table 3.1 ♦ Recognition of STG Print Ad Collage

	AMERICAS		
	United States	**Canada**	**Brazil**
Recognize IBM ad collage	63%	43%	32%
Correctly branded IBM	83%	77%	57%
Correct ad recall	53%	33%	18%
GRPs	403	English = 75 French = 63	42

performance measures for an STG print ad campaign that ran in the Americas (United States, Canada, and Brazil). In each country, we presented a collage of the print ads—debranded, as described previously—and asked research participants whether they recognized the images. Here we see that with the exception of Brazil, many respondents reported that they recognized the ads. In the United States, fully 63% of respondents claimed recognition. We can, of course, compare these numbers with norms that have emerged from our testing over time, and thus we have a very good sense of whether the ads are performing above or below expectations.

Also shown in Table 3.1 are percentages of respondents who, when asked, correctly branded the ad as IBM. Again, the U.S. column shows that 83% knew that IBM had produced the ads. This, in turn, means that 53% had correct ad recall for the campaign in the United States, as the third row of Table 3.1 shows. Finally, the table includes the number of GRPs for the campaign in each country.

In this instance, the U.S. numbers suggest that the campaign is quite successful, and we would have little reason to be concerned. In contrast, in Brazil, the numbers are not so positive. In such a case, we would look to various factors as potential reasons for the shortfall. Figure 3.10 shows some of the pieces of the advertising puzzle that must operate well individually for a complete advertisement to be successful.

Note that any one of the pieces of the overall puzzle can cause fail-ure in-market. That is, even if all five of the other elements are at or above threshold levels, if the message is not clear and relevant, the advertising will fail. Consider the case of the Brazil performance scores in Table 3.1. The ad investment to date in that country at the time of our survey, at 42 GRPs, may not be sufficient to produce suc-cess. A GRP of 42 could reflect that 42% of the target audience was exposed to the ad once, or it could mean that only 10% of the target audience saw the ad but were exposed to it, on average, 4.2 times. Thus, the element in Figure 3.10 termed "Right Investment" is a con-sideration that would warrant further investigation.

Indicators from other metrics in the AIM study often provide simi-lar insights. The information from Table 3.2, drawn from the same campaign analysis as the recognition data just reviewed, shows how our exposed versus unexposed analyses can shed light on advertising performance. In Table 3.2, which reflects campaign performance for parts of Europe, we summarize the results for the two key groups on most of the funnel-based metrics described previously. In the left-hand columns, we list the individual measurements, beginning with general awareness of the print and television ad executions, followed by brand image, consideration, preference, and FSE, respectively. The remaining columns provide performance results. Column A shows the scores for the exposed group, and column B shows the same scores

Figure 3.10 ♦ The Advertising Puzzle

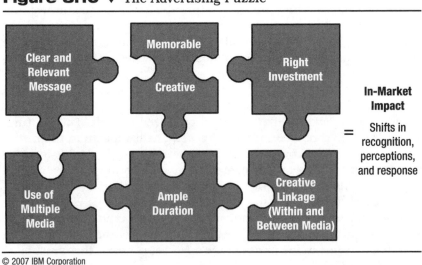

© 2007 IBM Corporation

Table 3.2 ♦ Exposed Versus Unexposed Analysis Results

		1Q07		
		Exposed to IBM Ads (A) (n = 113)	Not Exposed to IBM Ads (B) (n = 45)†	Difference Between Exposed and Not Exposed
TV	Unaided TV Ad Awareness	36% ▼	N/A	N/A
Print	Unaided Print Ad Awareness	78% ◄	N/A	N/A
Brand Image Attributes	Helping your company innovate	28%[B]	3%	+25
	Offering affordably priced products	14%[B] ◄	3%	+11
	Offering products that integrate easily	32%[B]	11%	+21
	Offering products that help simplify your infrastructure	24%	15%	+9
	Having relevant offerings that meet your needs	29%[B] ▼	9%	+20
	Being a leader in delivering infrastructure solutions	41%	29%	+12
	Helping create a more open or flexible infrastructure	31%[B]	11%	+20
Brand Consideration / Preference	Unaided Brand Consideration	66%[B] ◄	43%	+23
	Unaided Brand Preference	33% ◄	25%	+8
Favorable Selling Environment	**Overall Openness to Doing Business**	19%[B] ◄	4%	+15
	Recommend to a colleague	26%	31%	−5
	Seek out more info. about products/services	21%	22%	−1
	Meet or take a call with this company's sales reps	29%[B] ◄	4%	+25
	Identify yourself as interested	23%[B] ◄	8%	+15
	Ask colleagues about their opinions/experiences	17% ►	15%	+2
	Request a bid or proposal from this company	22%[B]	4%	+18

for the unexposed. The far-right-hand column shows the difference between columns A and B, with the positive numbers reflecting a higher score for the exposed and the negative numbers reflecting a higher score for the unexposed.

There are two notations in column A that we use to help interpret the findings. First, a superscript "B" appears next to any row percentage in the column that is significantly greater (from a statistical perspective) than the same-row percentage in column B. In these cases, exposed respondents are deemed to be significantly different from unexposed respondents. In addition, some columns contain an upward-facing or downward-facing triangle, which designates a trend up or down from the previous quarter's data. Advertisers at IBM monitor both indicators closely to gauge advertising performance and to determine how that performance changes over time.

The advertising campaign tested in Table 3.2 was deemed to be a success. Almost all the metrics were greater for the exposed population, and many of these were significantly greater. Of course, this analysis would have been repeated within customer sets to control for potential biases described previously.

It is notable that the approach described herein can be used to assess possible synergies between advertising media. Do our audiences react more favorably to IBM advertising when they have been exposed to two or more media platforms, such as print and Internet ads? Table 3.3 provides the results from one such investigation. In this case, we looked at our key metrics for four different subsets of our audience: (1) those exposed to both print and television ads, (2) those exposed to television ads only, (3) those exposed to print ads only, and (4) those exposed to no IBM ads. As Table 3.3 shows, there was a strong synergistic effect of the two media.

The Impact of Advertising on Bottom-Line Results

Up to this point, we have looked at only the survey metrics that emerge from IBM's AIM studies. These are important measurements because they confirm that our best ads have their intended effects, and they point to areas for improvement when we encounter challenges. However, marketing executives at IBM are interested in gaining insights into questions that have been at the forefront of advertising research for some time: Are our investments in advertising producing bottom-line results? What sort of return-on-investment (ROI) are we getting from our advertising?

A way to get at this issue at IBM is through a combination of AIM data and internal records. It occurred to us that we could look at rela-

Table 3.3 ◆ Key Metrics for In-Market Test

		Exposed to TV and Print (A) (n = 423)	Exposed to Only TV (B) (n = 40)[1]	Exposed to Only Print (C) (n = 312)	Not Exposed to TV or Print (D) (n = 154)
TV	Unaided TV Ad Awareness	100%	100%	N/A	N/A
Print	Unaided Print Ad Awareness	86%	N/A	60%	N/A
Brand Image Attributes	Helping your company innovate	33%C	35%	26%	28%
	Offering affordably priced products	19%BC	6%	12%	18%B
	Offering products that integrate easily	41%BC	21%	28%	35%B
	Offering products that help simplify your infrastructure	39%BCD	21%	31%D	22%
	Having relevant offerings that meet your needs	51%BCD	22%	33%	33%
	Being a leader in delivering infrastructure solutions	59%BCD	30%	50%BD	40%
	Helping create a more open or flexible infrastructure	38%BCD	14%	30%B	29%B
Brand Consideration / Preference	Unaided Brand Consideration	80%BCD	54%D	56%D	32%
	Unaided Brand Preference	30%CD	23%D	14%D	7%
Favorable Selling Environment	Overall Openness to Doing Business	32%BCD	11%	18%	21%
	Recommend to a colleague	35%BD	20%	36%BD	22%
	Seek out more info. about products/services	38%BCD	13%	29%B	28%B
	Meet or take a call with this company's sales reps	34%BCD	19%	27%	26%
	Identify yourself as interested	36%BCD	17%	26%	24%
	Ask colleagues about their opinions/experiences	33%	27%	29%	30%
	Request a bid or proposal from this company	37%BCD	17%	31%B	27%

tive revenues from companies at which decision makers had been exposed to our advertising versus companies at which decision makers were unexposed. We might expect that any differences would be lagged somewhat, as a result of sales cycles, but any revenue differences (within customer sets) would support the connection between advertising and ROI.

A challenge in this analysis was the important requirement that we not compromise the confidentiality or privacy of our AIM survey respondents. The survey is anonymous, and participants are ensured that their answers will be shared only in aggregate form. The following procedure was developed to make certain that all guidelines were followed. To do this, we worked closely with our research partner Marketing and Planning Systems Inc. (MaPS), which conducts two of the IBM AIM studies.

First, we had MaPS produce a database containing the Duns numbers (Dun & Bradstreet company identifiers) for companies that had responded to our survey. No survey response information was included in this database. Second, IBM analysts appended revenue data to the database and returned it to MaPS. Subsequently, MaPS merged the revenue data back to our AIM survey response database, and the appropriate analyses could proceed. MaPS conducted all its merge activities (and all its processing of AIM data) using only Duns numbers; thus, it never saw any company names for the survey respondents. In turn, IBM never saw individual company survey responses at all.

Using the new database, with company revenues appended, we could now look at relationships between advertising metrics from our AIM surveys and various business outcome measures, including purchase activity, total revenues, and share of wallet. The results have been illuminating and have enabled us to understand the impact of our advertising efforts as never before.

One of the first analytical efforts undertaken by the IMC Market Intelligence team was to look for evidence to support our belief that the FSE measures were related to business outcomes, as we had assumed from the outset. Figure 3.11 summarizes some of the results from one such investigation, an assessment of hardware purchasers in our IT AIM study.

We classified respondents into five different categories according to their composite FSE scores, as Figure 3.11 shows. We then looked at key revenue metrics associated with the FSE classifications. The top-most bar chart in Figure 3.11 shows that, in general, the higher the FSE score, the more likely respondent companies were to spend money with IBM. Although only approximately one-third of companies

Figure 3.11 ♦ Top-Line STG Results

STG

Percentage of Respondents

■ Without Revenue
■ Positive Revenue

FSE Score	0 - 2.67	2.68 - 4.83	4.84 - 6.50	6.51 - 8.00	8.01 - 10.00
Without Revenue	66%	71%	62%	54%	34%
Positive Revenue	34%	29%	39%	46%	66%

1. The probability that a company will have revenue with IBM increases with higher FSE levels.

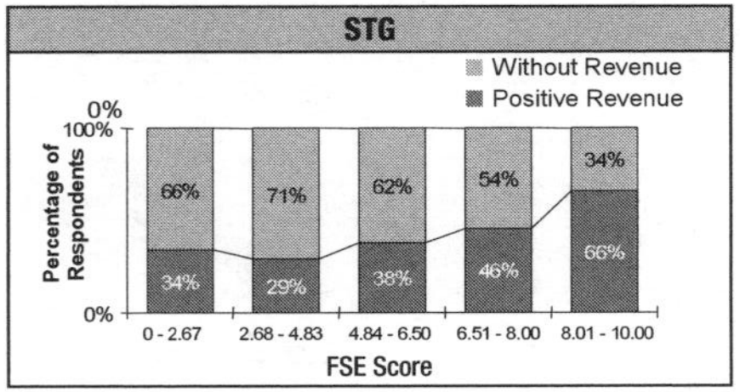

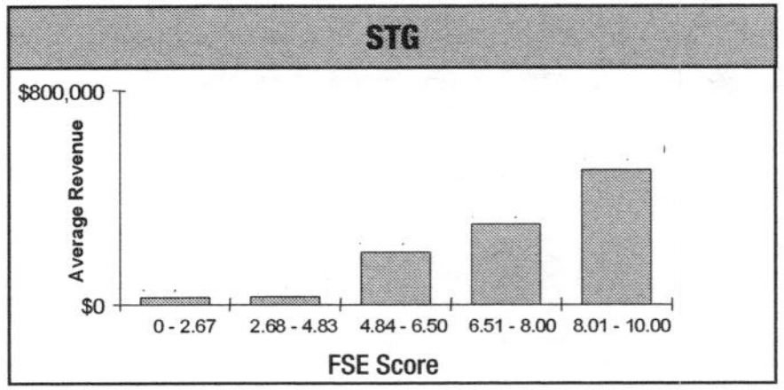

STG

Average Revenue

$0 — $800,000

FSE Score: 0 - 2.67, 2.68 - 4.83, 4.84 - 6.50, 6.51 - 8.00, 8.01 - 10.00

2. The higher the FSE score, the higher is the average spending.

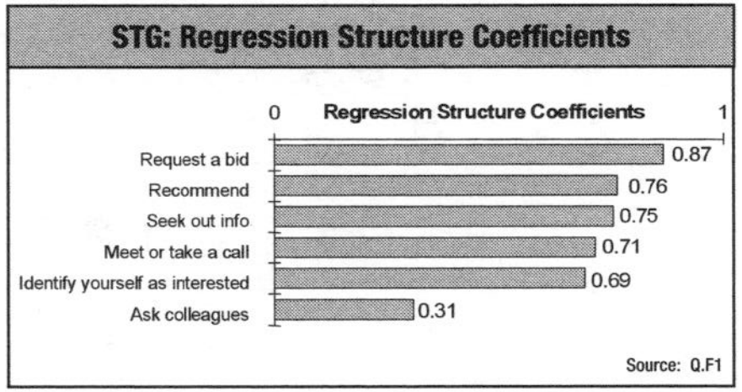

STG: Regression Structure Coefficients

Regression Structure Coefficients 0 — 1

Request a bid	0.87
Recommend	0.76
Seek out info	0.75
Meet or take a call	0.71
Identify yourself as interested	0.69
Ask colleagues	0.31

Source: 0.F1

3. All correlations between FSE items and revenue are statistically significant for STG.

4. The strongest predictor of STG revenue is "request a bid."

with FSE composite scores ranging from 0 to 2.67 purchased from IBM (within three calendar quarters of completing the survey), fully two-thirds of those with FSE composite scores between 8 and 10 had made purchases.

Among those who had made purchases, those with higher FSE scores spent more money with IBM, as Figure 3.11 also shows. In addition, regression structure coefficients indicate that willingness to request a bid from IBM on an upcoming IT project is most strongly associated with subsequent revenues. In total, these indicators led us to conclude that FSE was tied to positive business outcomes and that, in turn, advertising that had a positive influence on FSE scores would be beneficial to the company.

Still, it remained to be seen whether advertising could also be tied to these business outcomes. We decided to use structural equation modeling (SEM) to investigate the relationships between all key funnel metrics (including exposure to advertising) and bottom-line outcomes. Figure 3.12 shows the hypothesized model tested in our analysis. As Figure 3.12 shows, the model assumes a linear relationship among the funnel variables, flowing from left to right, such that exposure to IBM advertising can influence all other funnel variables, as well as business outcomes (e.g., revenues), both directly and indirectly. The brand image variable is hypothesized to influence business outcomes and all the funnel variables to its right, and so on.

Some variable definitions will help interpret the results of our SEM efforts. First, we should note that advertising was tested using two distinct approaches. For one model, we used a self-reported measure of television and print advertising exposure. Respondents had been asked in our AIM survey, "Now thinking about TV/print advertising, which, if any, companies that provide (category prompt) have you seen advertised on TV, or in a magazine or newspaper?" According to factor scores, they were coded roughly as .63 if they were aware of both IBM television and print, .33 if they were aware of only IBM television, .30 if they were aware of only IBM print, and 0 if they were aware of neither. The measure, termed "unaided ad awareness (TV + print)" in models reported subsequently, reflects the sum total exposure to IBM television and print advertising, as survey respondents reported.

We also ran models in which advertising exposure was coded according to respondents' recognition of selected ad campaign collages (as described previously). In this case, respondents who did not recognize the ad collage received a code of 0, those who recognized the ad collage (only) received a code of .5, and those who both recognized the collage and properly identified it as sponsored by IBM received a code of 1 (this variable is labeled "IBM IT ad exposure"). Thus, for our two

Figure 3.12 ♦ The Analytical Approach

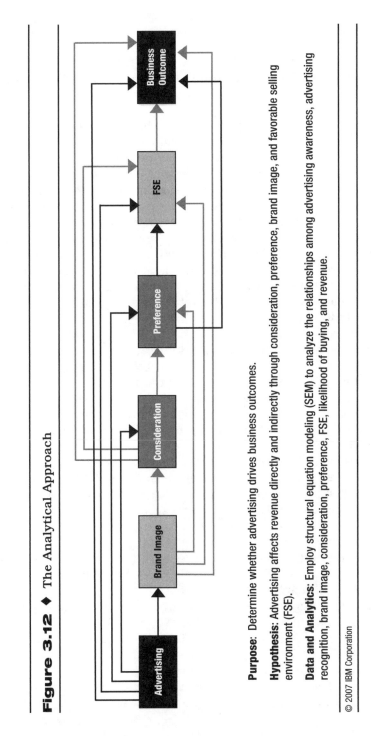

Purpose: Determine whether advertising drives business outcomes.

Hypothesis: Advertising affects revenue directly and indirectly through consideration, preference, brand image, and favorable selling environment (FSE).

Data and Analytics: Employ structural equation modeling (SEM) to analyze the relationships among advertising awareness, advertising recognition, brand image, consideration, preference, FSE, likelihood of buying, and revenue.

© 2007 IBM Corporation

ad exposure measures, one reflected exposure to specific campaigns, and the other reflected general exposure to IBM advertising.

Both brand image and FSE were composite factors that reflected responses to the items constituting those constructs. Consideration and preference were individual variables from the AIM surveys, as described previously.

Finally, we ran models testing several business outcomes, but two were of particular interest. First, we wanted to test whether advertising influenced the likelihood that respondent companies would become customers; that is, did those who reported exposure to IBM advertising subsequently spend (any) money with us? Thus, we used a business outcome measure, which we termed "purchase incidence," coded as 0 if no matching revenues were found for that company and coded as 1 if revenues were present. The second business outcome tested was the amount of spend, labeled "IT revenue." Analyses using this measure were restricted to customers only (i.e., those who had matching revenues in the database). In addition, to minimize the impact of especially large revenue totals at a few companies, we used Log(revenues) in our modeling.

Our initial models were restricted to U.S. data and to our IT audience surveys between the third quarter of 2006 and the second quarter of 2007, where the matching of AIM survey responses and revenue information proved most successful. Of the 1437 IT hardware respondents in the AIM survey, we successfully matched 1028 (72%) to our ledger data. For IT software respondents, we matched 999 of 1372 cases (73%). Only hardware and software revenues from the ledger data were included in the models.

Figure 3.13 shows the results of our model testing unaided ad awareness (TV + print), other funnel measures, and IT revenue. First, consideration and preference do not appear in this model, as they were dropped because they did not increase overall explanatory power. Second, advertising awareness has both direct and indirect effects on revenues. The direct effect coefficient is 1.457, as Figure 3.13 shows. There are two indirect effects. The first is that ad awareness has a significant influence on FSE (.512), which in turn influences revenues (.342) to produce an indirect effect of .175 (.512 ×.342). There is also an indirect path from ad awareness through brand image and FSE to revenues. This indirect path is 2.091 × .884 × .342 = .632. The total effect of ad awareness on revenues is the sum of direct (1.457) plus indirect (.175 + .632 = .807) effects, which adds to 2.264. The indirect effects account for slightly more than one-third of the total.

It is difficult to interpret the causal path coefficients directly because of the different scales used for the variables in the model. For

Figure 3.13 ◆ Effect of Unaided Ad Awareness on IT Revenue

Unaided TV and print ad awareness has a significant direct effect on IT revenue (1.457) and significant indirect effects through brand image and FSE.

Consideration and preference were dropped from the model for parsimony because they did not increase overall explanatory power.

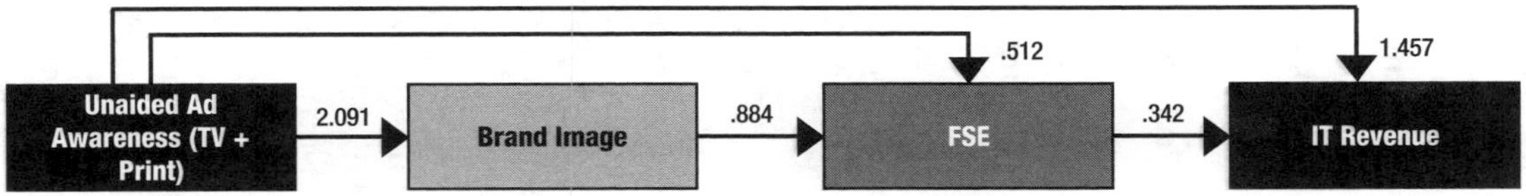

Path Model

Unaided ad awareness is a composite of unaided TV ad awareness (QA1) and unaided print ad awareness (QB1), scored as aware if respondent recalled either IBM TV or print advertising or unaware if neither.

Brand image is a factor comprising the following IT attributes (common across STG and SWG): helping your company innovate, offering products that help simplify your infrastructure, having relevant offerings that meet your needs, and helping create a more open or flexible infrastructure.

FSE is a factor comprising the following items: seek out more information, identify yourself as interested, ask colleagues about their opinions, meet or take a call, request a bid or proposal, and recommend to a colleague.

IT revenue is the average revenue across 3Q06 to 2007 for each company that participated in the AIM survey and was available in the IBM Ledger.

Notes: Only significant path coefficients are shown.
© 2007 IBM Corporation

this reason, we constructed a simulator, which enabled us to estimate the impact of possible increases in ad awareness on IBM revenues. Table 3.4 shows the predicted impact of 5%, 10%, and 15% increases in unaided ad awareness (TV + print) on key model variables.

Clearly, there are benefits that are likely to accrue with the increase of television and print advertising exposure. The challenge, of course, is to find the best ways to generate that increase, whether through the brute-force approach of buying additional media or through a strategic realignment of advertising across media outlets. However, the key is that now IMC decision makers at IBM have a gauge against which to set strategy.

Revenues Tied Directly to Advertising Campaigns

So far, we have looked only at a revenue model and only at the impact of self-reported exposure to television and print advertising. Now, let's consider the models based on exposure to specific campaigns, as determined by the recognition approach. Here, we report two models. The first model uses IBM IT purchase incidence as the primary business outcome, and the second uses IT revenue as the outcome variable.

Figure 3.14 shows the results of the SEM model that uses IT ad exposure as the key indicator of advertising influence and IT purchase incidence as the key business outcome. In this model, both consideration and preference contribute meaningfully to overall explanatory power and thus are included as part of the model. Moreover, it is preference that has the strongest direct influence on IT purchase incidence.

A notable aspect of the model depicted in Figure 3.14 is that there is no direct influence of IT ad exposure on purchase incidence. All influence is indirect, coming through the impact of ad exposure on other mediating variables in the model. When we sum the indirect effects, we find that the total effect of advertising is .053, which means that prospects who register and properly brand IBM television and/or

Table 3.4 ♦ Simulated Impact of Increases in Ad Awareness

Change in Unaided Ad Awareness	Resulting Change in Model Metric		
	Brand Image	FSE	Annual Revenues
5%	.1	.1	$62,000
10%	.2	.2	$130,000

© 2007 IBM Corporation

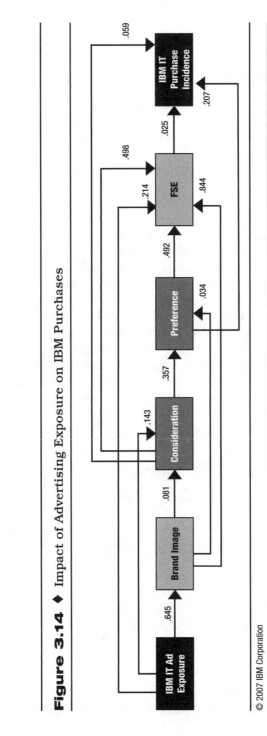

Figure 3.14 ◆ Impact of Advertising Exposure on IBM Purchases

© 2007 IBM Corporation

print advertising are 5.3% more likely than their counterparts to become customers.

Figure 3.15 shows the results of the model for IT revenues. Ad exposure does have a direct impact on revenues, with a coefficient of .477. In fact, the direct effects account for the bulk of the impact of advertising on revenues. Again using simulations, we were able to estimate that a 10% increase in exposure to the IT campaigns would generate an average annual gain of $68,000 per company.

A notable finding that emerged from our modeling exercises was that nearly all the positive influence on revenues comes from the portion of our ad-exposed audience who correctly branded the ad campaign as sponsored by IBM. Indeed, respondents who incorrectly branded the campaign as sponsored by an IBM competitor tended to have lower subsequent revenues than those who did not recognize the campaign at all. This, of course, leads us to adopt a strategy of increased exposure for ad campaigns with excellent brand affinity, but with a change to a strategy of rework for those campaigns that do not enjoy high correct branding.

There are many other ways to use this information about advertising's impact on bottom-line results. IBM managers can use these analyses to study advertising's effects on different segments of customers and prospects. Similarly, results in different geographic areas can help determine where investments in advertising are likely to pay dividends. In addition, we now have a way to estimate the bottom-line impact of added exposure to our advertising, which enables us to make informed decisions about the viability of those investments.

◆ SUMMARY COMMENTS

In this chapter, we have reviewed the basic research components that make up the ongoing program of advertising research at IBM. We have noted how the components are tied to different stages in the advertising development process, and we have emphasized how the application of best-in-class techniques, refined over time, provides unique insights into our investments in this marketing tactic.

However, we should not overlook two important aspects of advertising research that garner considerable attention at IBM. First, the standard components of our research program, described previously, are just part of the entire effort. Many other activities are implemented, as needed, to address other questions that arise from time to time. Second, we consider no insight valuable unless we can take actions as a result. IBM is committed to its advertising research and budgets a considerable sum each year to support the work, but there

Figure 3.15 ♦ Impact of Advertising Exposure on IBM Revenues

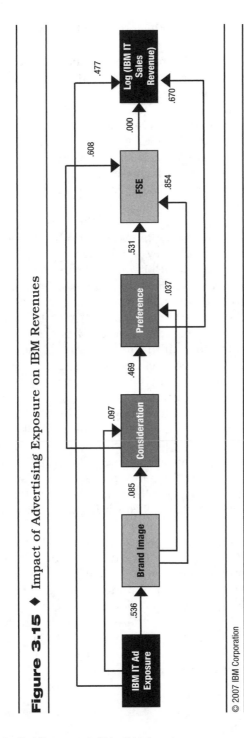

© 2007 IBM Corporation

is equal commitment to the follow-up activities that are based on our research findings.

Consider some of the ad hoc research that supplements the regular program of ad research at IBM. A good example is investigations into some of the emerging digital media and the opportunities to use such media to communicate important messages to our selected audiences. We have used various techniques to help us better understand interactive media. For example, we have deployed a variation on experimental designs to help assess the relative effectiveness of banner ads that we place on different Web sites. Visitors to the Web sites are randomly shown different ad executions (perhaps three levels: ad A, ad B, and a public service ad). The same visitors are invited to participate in a brief survey as they depart the Web site, and differences in the answers they give to the questions can be attributed to the different banner ads to which they were exposed.

Other examples include IBM's investments in emerging networks that combine aspects of regular television with interactive features of the Internet, as well as systematic investigations into the possibilities that exist for social networking and other Web 2.0–inspired technologies. A recent series of studies enlightened our IMC teams as to the potential for branded content in this space. All these activities necessarily occur outside the scope of our ongoing programs.

However, regardless of whether we draw research insights from programmatic or ad hoc projects, all insights must become impetus for specific actions taken at the company as a result. We make every effort to ensure that both short- and long-term ramifications are realized. Thus, for example, the results of a banner ad experiment at selected Web sites might lead to the selection of ad B over ad A after we have conducted key performance metrics. It is also important that we understand the reasons for the performance differences and that we incorporate this into the collective body of knowledge that IBM accrues over time.

In our ongoing research programs, this philosophy of pursuing business implications from our advertising research findings has been taken quite seriously. In our copy-testing efforts, for example, we have established a formal document of understanding, "Action Standards," with our IMC colleagues. Under this agreement, ads that do not meet performance thresholds (based on formulas and normative data) do not get rolled out into market without scrutiny. Depending on its scores, an individual ad execution can receive one of three grades: (1) ready for execution, as is; (2) acceptable for execution, given certain enhancements and/or adjustments; and (3) not acceptable for execution.

Our in-market performance evaluations, derived from AIM studies, also drive specific actions from the teams at IBM. Perhaps we discover that an advertising campaign is not performing in one country at the level it experiences in other countries where it runs—a not-too-uncommon outcome. The IMC in-country team is alerted, and the need for a "deep dive" is ascertained. The first step in this process is to inspect the advertising program in that country, as it has been executed to date. Taking into account the elements of the puzzle depicted in Figure 3.10, an assessment is made as to the likely source of the problem. If one or more pieces of the puzzle are deemed to be insufficient, plans are developed to address that shortcoming. If all pieces are considered adequate, alternative rationales for underperformance are sought. Perhaps economic conditions in the country cause undue influence; competitive pressures may be at fault. In such cases, factors that are beyond the direct control of the advertising team may dictate that a different ad strategy altogether be considered.

What should be clear from the discussion herein is that the development and execution of a complete program of advertising research is not a simple undertaking. At IBM we have realized that to make maximal use of the marketing budget, taking the steps necessary to ensure that advertising money is well spent is a wise investment indeed. Every aspect of advertising is tested, and often retested, so that our executives can make decisions with confidence. To date, through the systematic implementation of the principles and practices we have described, we have been able to effect a consistent, measurable improvement in our advertising. Both the advertising and the research program that supports it have demonstrated a positive ROI.

PART THREE

MARKETING MIX RESOURCE
ALLOCATION AND PLANNING:
REDEPLOYMENT APPLICATIONS

From an effectiveness perspective, the size of a company's marketing budget often matters less than how, where, when, and for what purpose it is spent. This is true for the entire marketing budget as well as the media budget. The two chapters in Part Three address the manner in which marketing mix analytics and data-driven econometric models have been applied to improve marketing mix decision making.

In "Optimal Allocation of Marketing Mix Resources: B2C and B2B Case Studies," University of Connecticut researcher V. Kumar presents case studies conducted at two *Fortune* 500 companies. The first case study focuses on questions pertaining to the overall marketing communications spend and the allocation of funds across vehicles at a consumer packaged goods company. The marketing budget had increased at a rate faster than the company's 10% annual revenue growth. Senior marketing executives were interested in reversing this trend and believed that marketing mix modeling could help in two respects: (1) determining whether the marketing spending level was optimal in terms of generating the maximum sales revenue and, (2) if not, identifying the optimal mix for future budget planning. Through a sales-response model, the most effective marketing variable was found in terms of maximum return on investment. The suggested optimal allocation of marketing spend ensured a $1.71 million revenue increase, in a given year, for one product category from reallocating resources across various media.

In the second case study, Kumar studies the customer acquisition and retention faced by a high-tech B2B manufacturer in the durable goods industry. This company was concerned with justifying its direct marketing expenses in terms of profitability and was looking for ways to improve return on investment by reallocating resources across each customer in each channel. Furthermore, too much emphasis was being placed on minimizing the costs of both acquisition and retention independently, thus ignoring the bigger picture of balancing acquisition and retention together. To help marketing managers make better allocation decisions, information about each prospect before acquisition and each customer after acquisition was collected. Using a forward-looking metric, such as customer lifetime value (CLV), it was found that the company was consistently overspending on low-CLV customers. Therefore, an optimal allocation strategy was applied to the company's business, and the results demonstrate the efficacy of this strategy.

In "Strategic Allocation of Marketing Resources: Methods and Insights," Venkatesh Shankar of Texas A&M University demonstrates how companies strategically allocate their resources within the marketing mix and between marketing mix variables and nonmarketing variables; across products, markets, and marketing channels; and over the product life cycle using a variety of marketing analytics. From the extant literature, Shankar presents a variety of marketing mix resource allocation processes couched in specific application settings. In addition, he describes three broad types of normative models for resource allocation: (1) a set of optimization rules applied to an econometrically estimated model, (2) empirical models that offer norms for strategic decision making, and (3) analytical models with or without empirical estimation of market-specific parameters. Managerially relevant insights gained from these models are highlighted.

When viewed together, the work of Kumar and Shankar alerts senior marketing executives and marketing research professionals to emerging methods and potentially fruitful research directions for marketing scholars and educators.

CHAPTER 4

Optimal Allocation of Marketing Mix Resources: B2C and B2B Case Studies

V. Kumar, University of Connecticut

◆ INTRODUCTION

The methods used to allocate marketing mix resources have shifted over the years as companies attempt to keep up with evolving technology. At a macro level, organizations now must market across several channels, including television, print, radio, direct mail, and public relations. This twenty-first-century trend is quite a change from trends at the turn of the twentieth century, when print advertisements in magazines, in newspapers, and on posters were the only means to communicate messages. It was not until the early 1920s that radio broadcasting became a second channel to allocate resources. This was later followed by the introduction of television in the 1940s and its emergence into a modern marketing trend in the 1950s. At this stage, the decision to allocate resources was still relatively simple because there were minimal distribution choices.

However, when cable television (1980s) and the Internet (1990s) came of age, the number of distribution channels exploded. Digital

The author thanks Roger Kerin and Rob O'Regan for their guidance and Bharath Rajan and Archana Muppaka for their assistance in the preparation of this article. The author also thanks Robert Leone for his comments and Renu for copyediting the first draft of this article.

advertising, including the use of Internet search engines such as Google to promote products and services, has revolutionized marketing. In addition to opening up a wealth of opportunities, however, the changing media landscape also poses great challenges for marketers.

In years past, the demographic profile of a particular media activity gave planners and marketing managers enough data to decide on allocating marketing dollars for each media activity. However, the current era requires media planners to be cognizant of all the microlevel changes in demographics and to decide, at a much more granular level, the appropriate ways to reach the right audience through the right media. With new media options opening up, media agencies are forced to rethink their marketing resource allocation strategies as to how and where to invest their marketing dollars. By developing a thorough understanding of market trends and looking at competitors' allocation strategies, marketers can take a microlevel approach as to which media is appropriate for each channel.

The following sections provide case discussions of a business-to-consumer (B2C) company in the packaged goods industry and a high-tech manufacturer of durable products in the business-to-business (B2B) industry, each of which has reallocated its marketing resources to ensure revenue maximization and efficient customer management.

♦ MARKETING MIX MODELING IN A B2C ENVIRONMENT

How should marketing dollars be allocated? This is the one question that concerns all marketing managers across all industry verticals. In general, marketing budgets are based on a percentage of the previous year's revenues or budget. Although such budgets are easy to create, they often fall short of achieving their targets. Specifically, managers often face a challenge when it comes to selecting the right media and the appropriate allocation of marketing spend into that media. The challenge lies in making marketing investments productive, as the failure to do so may lead to suboptimal business performance.

Consider the example of Colgate. The company's Total brand of toothpaste was supported with print, television, and online advertising. For this brand, Colgate wanted to know the optimal media mix to achieve its marketing goals. In other words, marketers wanted to increase the purchase intent of their target audience (adults, aged 18 to 49 years) who occasionally or never used Colgate Total. They intended both to identify the optimal media mix by measuring each medium's ability to increase purchase intent and to enhance key branding metrics, keeping their cost structure in focus.

To achieve this goal, Colgate undertook traditional testing methodology and analysis. Through this, the company determined the absolute gain that advertising causes for different branding metrics. It allocated more money to online efforts and then conducted return on investment (ROI) analysis, which studied the branding impact and dollars spent in each advertising medium. The data from Colgate showed that it cost 23% more to encourage consumer purchase using television alone than to do so using television in combination with online. Therefore, the solution for Colgate's multichannel campaign lay in reallocating marketing dollars to online advertising, which would be more cost effective at driving purchase intent and enhancing key branding metrics.

The results were encouraging. By allocating media dollars to online channels, the purchase intent of the Total brand increased significantly over a plan that used only television and print. In other words, by merely reallocating marketing resources (i.e., marketing dollars), the company achieved significant branding lifts without spending any additional marketing dollars (Interactive Advertising Bureau 2003).

Ensuring investment productivity often entails the use of econometric modeling, such as marketing mix models. Because marketing managers are increasingly interested in improving ROI, marketing mix models aid in improving firm profitability apart from developing a competitive edge for the company. Decisions based on ROI are crucial for any company because they provide a practical framework for allocating resources more efficiently. This case study of a B2C company provides an in-depth look into marketing mix models and ROI-based decision making.

Business Problem

Company A is a *Fortune* 100 consumer packaged goods (CPG) company with operations across several countries. For one of its major markets (defined at the country level), revenues were increasing at 10%, but its marketing spending was increasing at an even faster rate. Typically, marketing invests in activities such as advertisements through television and print media, trade promotions, public relations (PR), consumer promotions, distribution activities, and new product launches. Figure 4.1 shows the allocation distribution of Company A's current marketing expenditure.

From Figure 4.1, it is clear that television accounted for the majority of the spending. Furthermore, for Company A, it is given that marketing spending is the biggest cost after manufacturing cost. In addition, with respect to a particular brand of interest (herein referred

Figure 4.1 ♦ Allocation Distribution of Current Marketing Spending

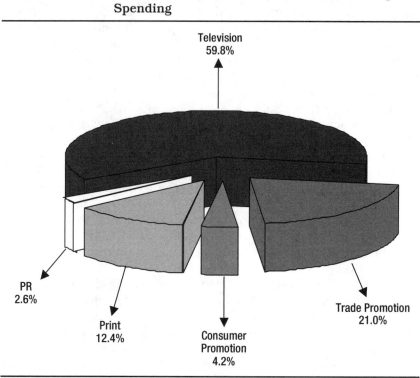

Television
59.8%

PR
2.6%

Print
12.4%

Consumer
Promotion
4.2%

Trade Promotion
21.0%

to as Brand X), a slight decrease in volume (of 5%) occurred in 2005 despite consistent growth of the product category.

With specific reference to television, other sources such as the Internet and digital video recorders (DVRs) were beginning to rival television as the primary media source among consumers. A 2007 IBM survey of consumer digital media and entertainment habits overwhelmingly suggests that personal Internet time rivals television time (IBM Consumer Study 2007). According to the study, conducted by the IBM Institute for Business Value, 19% of consumer respondents stated that they spend six hours or more per day on personal Internet usage, compared with 9% of respondents who spend six hours or more per day on television viewing. Across countries, 24% of U.S. respondents reported owning a DVR in their home and watching at least 50% of television programming on replay. In the United Kingdom, a vast majority of consumers surveyed use video-on-demand services (instead of owning a DVR), and fewer than one-third of U.K. consumers reported having changed their overall television viewing habits as a result of DVR ownership. In Australia, however, despite owning a DVR, most respondents prefer live television or replay less than 25% of their programming.

With this changing face of media, the CPG company began to rethink its marketing spending strategy. In essence, it wanted to know the dynamics of each of the marketing mix variables and whether it was spending the right amount in the right media. The company also wanted to know whether the current level of marketing spending was the optimal amount in terms of generating the maximum sales revenue. If not, the company wanted to know what that optimal mix would be. By making its marketing spend more effective, Company A believed that it would see a subsequent lift in product revenues.

Objectives of the Study

In this study, we worked with Company A to identify the variables that were driving sales, to measure those drivers, and then to reallocate resources across the marketing mix elements. To begin, an ROI analysis of marketing activities was performed to ascertain whether it was worthwhile to spend resources on a particular marketing activity. Return on investment was a key variable that led to answering questions with respect to the other variables for the different marketing activities. The ROI of each marketing activity was obtained by multiplying the corresponding volume response with the net revenue (NR) per sales unit in thousands (SUT) and dividing it by the cost of the marketing activity:

$$\text{ROI}_i = \frac{\text{SUTs per marketing activity}_i \times \text{NR/SUT}}{\text{Cost of marketing activity}_i} \times 1000.$$

With the generation of a demand model, the ROI for the different marketing activities was computed. The results are provided in Figure 4.2.

From Figure 4.2, it is clear that trade promotion and PR showed the maximum increase in terms of ROI in 2005. In contrast, television, print and consumer promotion performed poorly in both years. Currently, however, television receives the maximum share of marketing spending, approximately 60% (see Figure 4.1), even though its ROI was less than 1 (see Figure 4.2), which indicates a poor performance of the variable. In contrast, although PR received the least allocation of marketing spending, it generated the maximum ROI among all marketing variables. The disconnection between the allocation of resources for current marketing spending and ROI creates a strong case for studying the drivers of sales as they relate to marketing resource allocation. Similarly, another finding that emanates from the

Figure 4.2 ◆ ROI for Different Marketing Activities

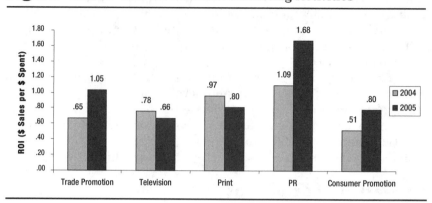

ROI figures for the different marketing activities is the reverse trend of ROI decreasing for television and print variables. This clearly indicates that the two variables have not performed efficiently, even though the company had allocated sufficient resources to them.

Although the immediate reaction based on these two observations would be to reduce marketing spending on those variables with ROI less than 1, marketers should exercise caution before doing so. The respective volume generation performance of both areas should be ascertained before deciding on cutting marketing dollars in either. Figure 4.3 depicts how various marketing activities contributed to the overall sales volume of Company A for Brand X.

Figure 4.3 shows that the marketing contribution increased over the two years, with trade promotion showing the maximum increase. This illustration clearly indicates that though television and print performed poorly on the ROI front and posted a reverse trend, they contributed the highest amounts in terms of volume contribution by marketing activity (18.2% by television and 4.2% by print for 2005). Therefore, it is clear that the marketing dollars cannot be reduced from these two variables simply because they have poor ROI. This leads to the obvious question: Can we optimally allocate the resources across variables in such a manner that would maximize profitability?

This finding shows that there is enough scope to move money across the categories. By developing new insights into the poorly performing variables in its marketing mix, the company would be able to reallocate resources across the buckets on the basis of ROI and to optimize the spending of marketing activities.

The next step was to find the volume contribution of each variable. To estimate the demand model, information about the country under

Figure 4.3 ◆ Volume Contribution by Marketing Activity

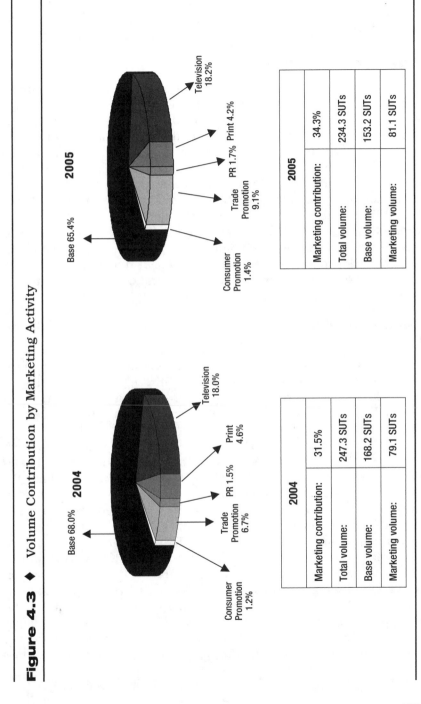

2004

Base 68.0%

Television 18.0%

Print 4.6%

PR 1.5%

Trade Promotion 6.7%

Consumer Promotion 1.2%

2004	
Marketing contribution:	31.5%
Total volume:	247.3 SUTs
Base volume:	168.2 SUTs
Marketing volume:	79.1 SUTs

2005

Base 65.4%

Television 18.2%

Print 4.2%

PR 1.7%

Trade Promotion 9.1%

Consumer Promotion 1.4%

2005	
Marketing contribution:	34.3%
Total volume:	234.3 SUTs
Base volume:	153.2 SUTs
Marketing volume:	81.1 SUTs

study, market characteristics, available data, and the study approach is necessary. The following section gives a brief outline about the required information.

Background Information

There are five territories in the country of study, which we number 1–5. The channel examined in the study includes only grocery. The study was conducted with the data collected from two major retail chains—which we call Retail Chain 1 and Retail Chain 2—that control more than 75% of the market share in this category. Although the principal interest was in Brand X, the analysis also considered four competing brands: Brands Y, Z, A, and B. Among the four competitors for which data were available, the focus of study was on Brand Y and Brand Z. Brand Y has 18 different stockkeeping units (SKUs), and Brand Z has seven different SKUs, and the brand under consideration, Brand X, also has seven different SKUs. Brand Y dominates the competition landscape in the product segment under study with 110 SUT in the 2005 calendar year. However, Brand Z shows the highest growth in this segment (52%) in 2005 with 42 SUT.

Data Availability

At the beginning of the study, data to conduct the analysis were available from five categories: (1) scanner, (2) media, (3) PR, (4) trade promotion, and (5) weather. For Brand X, SKU-level scanner data were available for the two retail chains and five territories where the particular brand was sold. Figure 4.4 provides a snapshot of the data description.

The data are available as weekly and monthly observations over three years. Because the purpose of the project was to model sales volume response at the retail chain–territory level over time, the structure of the data is cross-sectional, and time-series data were available for a period from August 2002 to November 2005. The period from December 2002 to November 2005 was considered for model estimation. Thus, there were 156 weeks of observations for each retail chain within each territory. Most of the marketing mix variables were observed at the retail chain–territory level. However, for variables for which data were available at the national or territory level, observations were repeated across all retail chain territories or across retail chains for each week. The data structure was conducive to include interaction between marketing mix variables and retail chain–territory dummies so that the retail chain–territory effects could be captured.

Figure 4.4 ◆ Data Description

Figure 4.4 ◆ Data Description

DATA SOURCES

Scanner Data

Information Obtained

- Volume (baseline & category) at the national, retail chain, and SKU level
- Value (baseline & category) at the national, retail chain, and SKU level
- Distribution (weighted) at the SKU level varying over retail chain territory
- Price at the SKU level varying over retail chain territory

Media Data

Information Obtained

- Television and Print TARPs obtained from campaigns at the territory level
- Print advertising done through magazines and newspapers, obtained at territory and national levels

PR Data

Information Obtained

- The weighted PR data were divided into 2 groups. One weighted with new factors, such as visual appeal, significance of the medium, and size, and one weighted with readership and/or population. Both groups were examined at the national and territory level

Trade Promotion Data

Information Obtained

- From promotion weeks (PW) for each SKU at the retail chain level, variables such as promotion depth (PD) and promotion breadth (PB) were obtained

Weather Data

Information Obtained

- Weather-related data such as maximum temperature, minimum temperature, average rainfall, and average sunshine hours were available at the national level

Consumer Promotion Data

Information Obtained

- Sampling data were available at the territory level

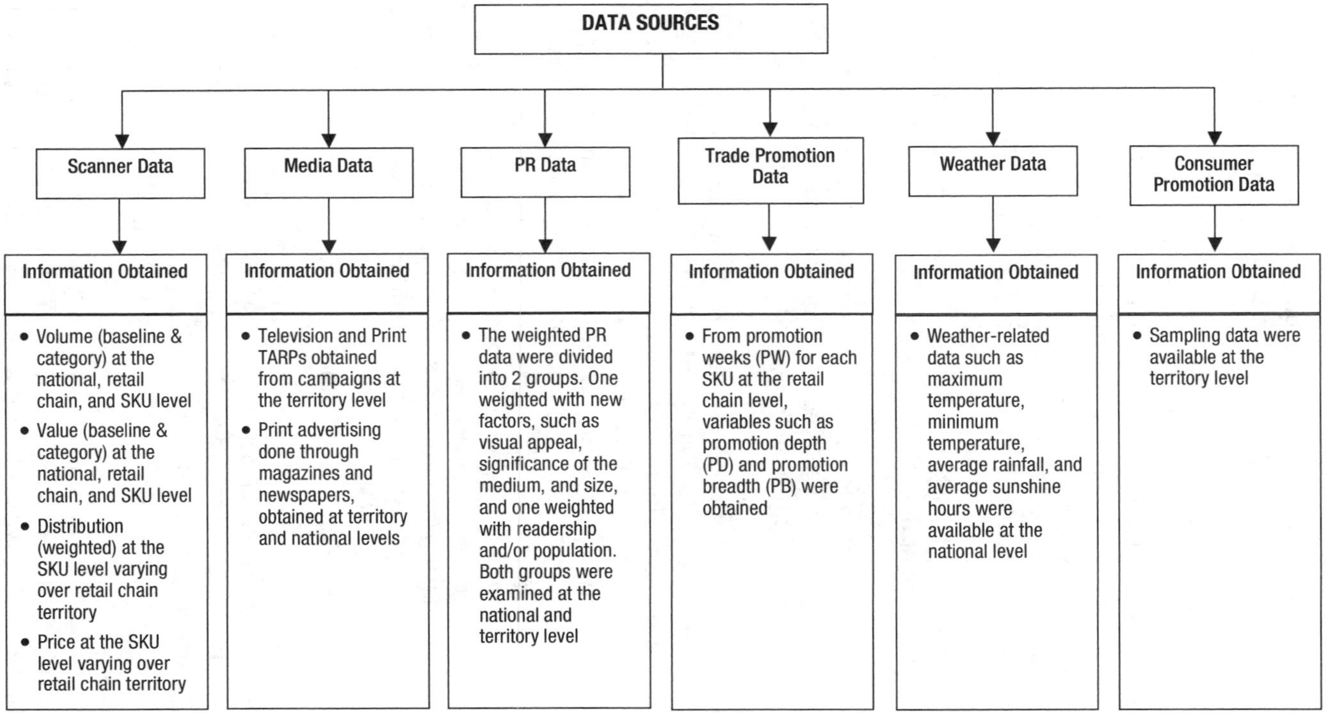

Study Approach

This section describes the execution of the study in light of the business problem, the study objectives, and the data availability.

Method used. Marketing spending is largely an expense rather than an investment. Although it is essential to spend more to sell more, companies must establish benchmarks to get the best return on the spending. Furthermore, it is required that all costs in marketing spending that do not add consumer value or build shareholder value be eliminated. In all, the gap between marketing spending and revenues must be reduced. Marketing mix modeling is the tool that will help achieve this objective.

A general form of the typical simplified marketing mix model is provided in Equation 1:

(1) Sales = function (e.g., price, distribution, television advertising, print advertising, trade promotions, consumer promotion, competitive activity).

Estimate the demand model. To bring to light the relationship between different marketing mix elements and the firm's sales volume, various functional forms of models were explored to arrive at the best model that could most accurately do so. Because Company A deployed several marketing programs at the same time, the demand model was carefully tested for interaction effects between different marketing elements.

To find the solution to the resource allocation problem through the data provided, the data needed to be prepared for modeling purposes. The following section provides the various types of data that were provided and the type of data transformation that was done to them.

Data Transformation

Typically, three types of transformation were performed with the independent variables: (1) lag, (2) log, and (3) square. In this model, different transformations were applied to different groups of variables. The variables are explained below.

Pricing

In this study, because price is the only marketing variable that directly determines revenue, it is among the most important elements of the marketing mix. Two types of price were used in the model: a base price and an average price. These were calculated for each SKU as follows:

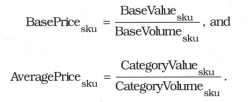

$$BasePrice_{sku} = \frac{BaseValue_{sku}}{BaseVolume_{sku}}, \text{ and}$$

$$AveragePrice_{sku} = \frac{CategoryValue_{sku}}{CategoryVolume_{sku}}.$$

The base price was included as an independent variable in the model, and the average price was used to calculate the promotion depth (PD). The combined base price for the top three SKUs was also calculated, as the total base value for the top three SKUs divided by the total base volume for top three SKUs. The formula for the combined base price is as follows:

$$\frac{\Sigma(BasePrice \times BaseVolume_{sku})}{\Sigma\, BaseVolume_{sku}}.$$

Distribution

In the analysis, weighted distributions were used to predict the sales volume; therefore, the weighted distributions for all SKUs were obtained. Because it was suspected that the weighted distributions of the SKUs have different effects on the sales volume in different territories, interaction terms of these variables were created with the retail chain–territory dummies.

Promotion

The information on number of promotion weeks (PW) for each SKU was available in the data. To examine the interaction between promotion and distribution, data were transformed to obtain promotion breadth (PB) at the SKU level. Depending on the values of PD, the PBs were divided into four categories and each category was again divided among the two retail chains. Therefore, we have eight different PBs for each SKU.

The promotion depth is calculated as the difference between the base price and the category price divided by the category price. The PB of the SKU is the product of PD and the weighted distribution of the SKU.

Television Advertising

The most commonly discussed advertising-response curve shapes are concave and S shaped. Prior research suggests that advertising response models comprise three major components: shape, dynamics, and interaction.

1. Shape is the long-term level of sales expected at each level of advertising. Such relationships may be linear or S shaped. In Company A's case, the relationship has been S shaped; therefore, television total advertising rating point (TARP) values were transformed according to an S shape.

2. Dynamics refers to the rate of sales increase when advertising is increasing and to the rate of decay when adverting is decreasing; therefore, the decay constant and parameters of the S-shaped curve control the dynamics.

3. Interaction investigates the type of market that is more appropriate for advertising and the appropriate structure of the interaction of advertising with other elements of the marketing mix. Therefore, the S-shaped transformed television TARPs was crossed with retail chain–territory dummies to determine which market was more responsive to television. In addition, the interaction of television advertising with print advertising was also examined.

Print Advertising

For print advertising, the quarterly data were transformed to weekly data to match the data structure. Because it was necessary to consider the decay effects of print TARPs within the quarter, more print TARPs were allocated at the beginning of a week and less in the following weeks.

Consumer Promotion (Sampling)

It was suspected that sampling had a lagged effect on consumers' buying decisions. Therefore, 12 lagged terms of sampling were created. Because it was not known how sampling would influence sales volume, log transformations and square transformations of the variables were also created to examine which transformation fit the data better. Some interactions of sampling and retail chain–territory dummies were also created.

Launch

The sales volume for the week when a product is launched is likely to be greater than that in the weeks following the launch. Therefore, dummy variables were created to determine whether there was a significant effect of this event on sales volume. Because the launch might have a lagged effect, lags of the dummies were also created. Furthermore, because the effects of product launch might be different in different retail chains and territories, the interactions of product launch with retail chain–territory dummies were also created.

PR

The PR data were weighted with the following factors: visual appeal, significance of the medium, and size. Different weights were assigned to the factors according to their influence on the effectiveness of PR. For different levels of visual appeal and significance of the medium, different numbers were assigned to represent their effects. Another set of weighted PRs were also calculated with weights based on readership and/or population.

Competition

In addition to Brand X variables, the effects of competitors' base price, PB, distribution, and television TARPs on Brand X's sales volume were also examined. The competitors' base price was calculated in the same way as Brand X's base price. Similarly, competitors' PB was calculated in the same way as Brand X's PB. For competitors' television TARPs, the same S-shaped transformation was performed as for Brand X's television TARPs.

Halo Effect

The halo effect is the effect of other products in the product line on Brand X's sales volume. Seven important variables were included in the analysis to account for the halo effect. These variables were transformed to describe the S-shaped relationship in the same way as for the television advertising variables. The transformed variables were then interacted with the retail chain–territory dummies.

Thus, the final model had independent variables from all the groups: launch (initiatives), sampling (consumer promotion), trade promotion, PR, print advertising, television advertising, competition, and halo effect.

Data sets were created to evaluate the predictive accuracy of the in-sample and holdout-sample models. The in-sample method included all the observations in the first 135 weeks (December 2002 to June 2005), and the out-of-sample method included the observations for the previous 21 weeks (July 2005 to November 2005). The estimated parameters from the main regression were used to define the predicted dependent variable for both in-sample and out-of-sample data. For the overall model results (between December 2002 and November 2005), the R-square was found to be 95.8%, which indicates a good fit of the model with the data. For the estimation sample, the R-square was found to be 95.4%, indicating a good fit of the model with the data. With regard to the holdout sample (between July 2005 and November 2005), the mean absolute percentage error was found to be 7.8%.

Because the model was predicted with accuracy, the next step was to use the model results to answer the specific business the company had. These questions are answered in the following section.

Key Business Questions

The variables identified as having the most impact on sales were television, print, PR, trade promotion, and consumer promotion. With these marketing mix variables and some budget constraints, a multimodal optimization model was used to optimally allocate marketing resources across marketing activities. According to this allocation, it was suggested that expenditure on trade promotion, print, and PR be increased, whereas expenditure on television and consumer promotion be reduced.[1] Such a movement of spending generated additional revenue of $1.71 million for Company A for Brand X. Figure 4.5 shows the side-by-side comparison of current and optimized marketing spending.

With the major objectives of the study answered, the company then set out to address some specific business questions, which it answered with the help of the marketing mix model. For example, with specific reference to television, the company wanted to know how much to advertise and the duration of such exposures; in other words, would a 20-second commercial generate the same response as a 30-second spot? Likewise, the company wanted to know whether print had any impact on television advertising. If so, marketing could group the activities together to create a bigger impact and to optimize the dollars spent on each activity. The questions are discussed in the following sections.

Optimal Number of TARPs per Week

Two important questions are as follows: (1) What is the optimal number of TARPs per week? and (2) Do 20-second copies generate as much response as 30-second copies? Figure 4.6 shows the optimal number of TARPs per week.

The S-shaped volume response curve illustrated in Figure 4.6 shows that the threshold level is 20 TARPs per week, saturation occurs beyond 130 TARPs per week, and the optimal level seems to be 90 TARPs per week. To maximize volume, it is recommended that the increase can go up to just below 130 TARPs per week.

With regard to the response generated by the copies, 30-second copies generate 35% greater volume than 20-second copies. However, because the cost of a 20-second advertisement is only 60% of the 30-second advertisement, an ROI of 20-second versus 30-second copies must be evaluated.

Figure 4.5 ♦ Comparison of Current and Optimized Expenditure by Marketing Activity

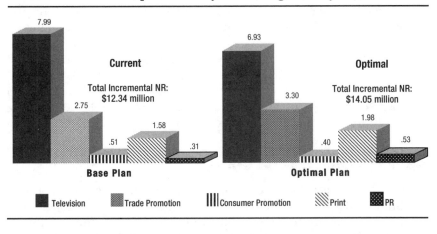

Figure 4.6 ♦ Optimal Number of TARPs per Week

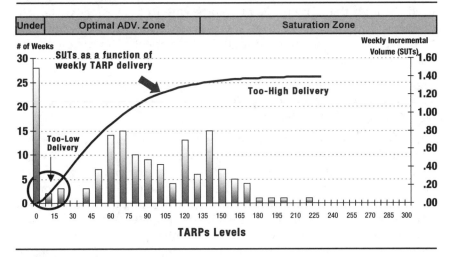

Have Ad Campaign 1 and Ad Campaign 2 for Brand X Experienced Wear-Out?

To calculate the wear-out effect for Ad Campaign 1 and Ad Campaign 2, the number of weeks the campaigns was on air was calculated. A dummy was created if the period is the first half of the weeks on air and 0 if otherwise. This dummy variable was included with the television advertising variables, and the new variable was added into the main model. The regression results showed that the interaction of television advertising with the dummy is not significant, which implies that there is no wear-out effect. Two separate regressions were performed for two different television campaigns: one for Ad Campaign 1 and the other for Ad Campaign 2. Given the following empirical findings, it was apparent that Ad Campaign 1 and Ad Campaign 2 had not experienced wear-out: (1) Volume response for the first half of campaign was not significantly different from the second half of campaign for both Ad Campaign 1 and Ad Campaign 2, and (2) volume response is comparable to other copies rated "normal."

Is There an Opportunity to Optimize Television Spends Using a Halo Effect?

There were several halo effect variables, which were significant in the final model. Because of their impact on the volume response, it can be said that there is an opportunity to optimize Brand X television spend through the halo effect of television advertising from Brand Y and Brand Z. Table 4.1 shows the effects of the halo effect variables on sales volume for 2004 and 2005. Such effects are measured through the percentage of volume due to halo effect variables. In Table 4.1, it is clear that there is an opportunity to optimize Brand X television spends through the halo effect of television advertising from SKUs 1 and 2.

Because We Can Buy Media per Territory, if We Face a Television Budget Cut, Which Territories Should We Prioritize?

The volume responses of television advertising by territory were calculated. The variables were grouped by territory rather than by campaign. Because all the television variables in the model were compared with the retail chain–territory dummies, identification of territory-specific variables was easy. Following this, the weighted volume response was calculated for each territory. With the average volume response TARPs (SKUs per 100 TARPs), it was found that Territories 1, 2, and 3 were significant. Therefore, those territories should be prioritized.

Does Print Advertising Have Any Impact on the Effectiveness of Television Advertising?

Both television and print are major advertising channels. It was suspected that they would generate a greater effect by interacting with each other than if they operated independently. To test whether the

Table 4.1 ♦ Opportunity to Optimize Television Spends Using Halo Effect

	2004	2005
Contribution of Halo Effect to Overall Sales Volume	5.3%	8.7%

interaction between print advertising and television advertising is significant, the interaction terms were created. For print variables, only the national-level magazine category provided enough observations, so only the interactions of national magazines with television campaigns were created. Figure 4.7 illustrates the impact of print advertising on television advertising. It was found that print advertising helps improve the effectiveness for three television campaigns only marginally. Therefore, there is no strong evidence of print advertising having a consistent impact on the effectiveness of television advertising.

Is There a Need to Have Different Trade Strategies for Retail Chain 1 and Retail Chain 2? What Discount Levels Work Best with Each?

To compare the different trade strategies of the two retail chains, the number of weeks on promotion for the three top SKUs in each of the three years was considered. The volume response for each retail chain for the three years and PW were known. Then, the volume responses per week for Retail Chain 1 and Retail Chain 2 for each year were calculated. The result showed that Retail Chain 1 generated greater volume lift than Retail Chain 2 as a result of promotion.

To find out the appropriate discount levels, a look into the standardized coefficients of Retail Chain 1 and Retail Chain 2 was necessary. From the standardized estimates, it was found that for Retail Chain 2, the discount level of 3%–13% was the optimal solution, whereas the discount level of 8%–8% worked the best for Retail Chain 1. Table 4.2 shows the discount levels that work best for the two retail chains.

Except for 2004, Retail Chain 1 promoted more often that Retail Chain 2 in the past three years. Furthermore, owing to promotions, Retail Chain 1 shows greater volume lift than Retail Chain 2. Therefore, there seems to be a significant difference in trade promotion effectiveness for Retail Chain 1 and Retail Chain 2.

Figure 4.7 ♦ Impact of Print Advertising on Television Advertising

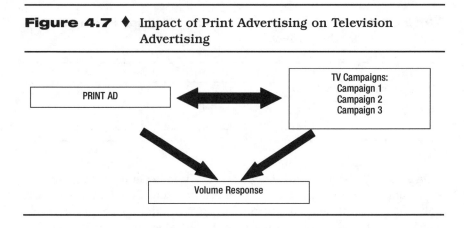

How Do We Compare with Competition on Discount Depth and Discount Weeks?

Discount depth refers to the extent to which Company X and the competition provides discounts. Discount weeks are the number of weeks that the discounts are in effect. Table 4.3 provides the comparison of competition between discount weeks and discount depth. Table 4.3 makes it clear that Brand X is the top promoter in terms of promotion depth and Brand Y is the top promoter in terms of promotion frequency.

Who Is the Key Competitor of Brand X?

After the key concerns were answered through this analysis, the company had an overarching question: Who was its biggest competitor with respect to Brand X? To answer that question, the sales volume for each of the four main competitors in 2003, 2004, and 2005 was considered. Brand Z was found to have the highest sales volume among Brand X's competitors, whereas Brand Y showed the strongest growth. After answering all the critical business questions, the next step was to optimize the marketing costs to maximize firm profitability. The next section describes the process.

Optimizing Marketing Cost to Maximize Profitability

The extent by which the marketing mix model output can be used to optimize the supply side depends on the boundary conditions imposed by the firm. For this project, Company A was interested in knowing whether it could achieve incremental sales by merely reallocating the

Table 4.2 ♦ Discount Levels for Retail Chains 1 and 2

For Retail Chain 1	8–18%
For Retail Chain 2	3–13%

Table 4.3 ♦ Discount Depth and Discount Weeks

Variable	Brand X	Competition	
		Brand Y	Brand Z
Promotion Week	25.0%	42.3%	21.2%
SKUs	7	7	18
Average Promotion Depth	13%	9%	11%

Brand X is the top promoter in terms of promotion depth

Brand Y is the top promoter in terms of promotion frequency

marketing budget across different marketing activities while keeping the overall marketing budget constant. In addition, the extent of change in the marketing budget for a particular marketing activity because of reallocation of the budget could not exceed 20% as compared with the previous year's budget. With these stringent constraints, advanced multimodal optimization techniques were used to show how Company A could generate an additional $1.71 million of incremental revenue for Brand X for one year through mere reallocation of the marketing budget across its marketing activities.

Key Learnings

Some of the key learnings from the study conducted include the following:

♦ The most effective media is measured in terms of maximum ROI. For example, in the case of television advertisements, maximum ROI was generated with between 50 and 90 TARPs per week for Brand X.

♦ Distribution of revenues is a dynamic process.

♦ Territorial differences were observed to be significant. For example, Territories 1 and 2 had consistently recorded TARPs in television advertising for three years.

♦ The effects across retail chains were found to be significant. For example, with respect to trade promotion effectiveness, a significant difference was observed between Retail Chain 1 and Retail Chain 2.

From this case study, it is clear that Company A faced a business problem by way of increased marketing costs that did not match the increase in sales revenues. Furthermore, the company was not sure about which marketing programs were the key drivers of sales and whether an optimal marketing mix structure was possible. Looking into this problem, the ROI of the various marketing mix variables was the first step taken. Through this, it was observed that the television, print, and trade promotion variables did not record an ROI that was greater than 1. This meant that the resources spent on these variables were not helping the company by way of increased sales revenues. Thus, the company decided to concentrate on these variables to optimize its marketing spend.

Specifically, with respect to television, the company was not sure whether to adopt a 20-second or a 30-second ad campaign. The rationale behind this question was that if a 20-second campaign generated as much response as a 30-second campaign, the company could reduce costs by switching to 20-second campaigns. Similarly, another unknown was the effectiveness between two ad campaigns. Knowing the answer would mean using one campaign rather than both, which would further optimize marketing costs. The other decisions related to television were whether television experienced the halo effect and which territories should be prioritized if television budgets were reduced. Other relevant questions included whether to have different trade strategies for their two key retail chains and what discount structures worked best for them.

In assessing the inefficiencies faced by a company, as well as the scope of reallocation of resources, three key factors emerge: (1) ROI versus spending level, (2) growth in ROI versus growth in spending level, and (3) volume contribution from different media spending. The three factors emerge from a larger concern of the company: how to optimize marketing spend to maximize revenue, which the company achieved through marketing mix modeling. Through such a model, the most effective marketing variable was found in terms of maximum ROI. The suggested optimal allocation of marketing spends ensured a $1.71 million revenue increase from reallocating the resources across various buckets. Therefore, this case study shows that optimal resource allocation can maximize a company's revenue proposition.

◆ MARKETING RESOURCE ALLOCATION IN A B2B ENVIRONMENT

In the past few years, new technologies and applications have been created to assist companies in managing their interactions with customers, including measurement of the effectiveness of different media on those interactions. This is not as straightforward as it sounds, however. There is the issue, for example, of which measure of effectiveness is most relevant: awareness, attitude, intention, sales, share, profit, and so on. The discipline of a one-to-one customer strategy has been applied more naturally to B2B situations than to B2C scenarios. In selling to other businesses, companies have always employed the principles of feedback, relationship building, and customization.

Let us consider the following as an example: Convergys, an outsourcer of inbound and outbound call center services, found that its previous emphasis on client acquisition was yielding diminishing sales. However, a new account development strategy—in other words, trying to sell more and better services to existing clients—turned out to be more challenging than anticipated. Ranking clients by their value to Convergys was difficult enough, but putting a new relationship-based sales and marketing strategy in place meant reengineering the structure and compensation of the sales force itself (Peppers and Rogers 1993).

For example, by focusing only on revenue growth without emphasis on cost management, Convergys would fail to maximize profitability. What it needed was an approach that would balance both revenue growth and cost management, creating market-based growth while carefully evaluating the profitability and ROI of marketing investments. Optimal allocation of resources and efforts across profitable customers and cost-effective and customer-specific communication channels (i.e., marketing contacts) are the keys to the success of such an approach. This calls for assessing the value of individual customers and employing customer-level strategies based on customers' worth to the firm. Thus, there is a need for a metric that will be an objective measure of future profitability of the customer to the firm (Berger and Nasr 1998). Customer lifetime value (CLV) is such a metric, as it takes into account the total financial contribution (i.e., revenues minus costs) of a customer over its entire lifetime with the company and therefore reflects the future profitability of the customer.

Common Business Problem

Each year companies spend millions of dollars on advertising to try to acquire new customers. With an increased ability to collect and analyze data that include each customer's purchase behavior and demographic information, firms are now able to better customize marketing campaigns to individual customers and to increase the overall effectiveness of those campaigns. However, evidence shows that many firms are still struggling to justify their direct marketing expenses in terms of profitability (Bachman 2007).

There are four main reasons for this dilemma. First, companies are not properly allocating the right resources between customer acquisition and retention. Second, firms don't understand how much to allocate across each customer in each channel among retained customers. Third, firms place too much emphasis on minimizing costs of both acquisition and retention. Fourth, managers are often too quick to try to maximize each stage of the acquisition and retention process, thus failing to look at the bigger picture of balancing acquisition and retention together. This, in turn, means that they focus on just one aspect of customers rather than managing the entire customer relationship.

To help marketing managers make better allocation decisions, we gathered information about each prospect before acquisition and each customer after acquisition, as follows: date of each purchase, number of proactive manufacturer-initiated marketing campaigns before that date, and type of campaign (i.e., face-to-face, telephone, e-mail, and Web).

We classified channels of communication into the following contact modes: rich (e.g., face-to-face, trading event meetings), standardized (e.g., direct mail, telephone), and e-mail/Web based (Reinartz, Thomas, and Kumar 2005). We expected the relationships between different channels of communication and predicted customer activity to be different. We needed to analyze customer responses separately across different channels because the costs of serving customers across different channels are different, and customers might exhibit different responsiveness across various channels. The costs of communication in each channel can influence managers' frequency of communication in each channel.

Face-to-face communications and trading event meetings are the richest and most direct means of communication possible among channel members. Relational customers tend to have high commitment and trust with their suppliers, which results in less uncertainty, more cooperation, and less complexity in their relationships than those with transactional customers (Reinartz, Thomas, and Kumar 2005). Rich modes of communication are preferred to standardized modes when issues in the channel structure are complex and when there is a high degree of uncertainty in the relationship. Rich modes of communication are also effective in converting transactional customers to relational ones.

Direct mail and telephone communication are the most standardized modes of individual-level communication available to an organization. Standardized modes are also the most cost-effective method for identifying customers who are interested in an organization's current promotion. For transactional customers, direct mail can be used in combination with telephone sales to generate interest in products while improving ROI. For relational customers, direct mail serves to maintain commitment and trust by communicating relationship benefits and to inform the best customers about new product offerings. Therefore, although the purpose of standardized communication may be different for transactional customers than for relational ones, we expect that the marginal response for increased frequency is the same across segments.

We expected that an optimal level of contact time exists between suppliers and buyers. Higher levels of previous communications lead to trust with the supplier and act as glue that holds together a communication channel. To maximize the effect of each contact, supplier firms need to pace their communication schedule to suit customer needs, whereas e-mail\Web-based contacts should be analyzed separately from other communication channels because Web-based communication is customer initiated (i.e., a passive mode of operation for the supplier).

However, there are several advantages to tracking Web-based contacts in a B2B setting. First, Web-based communication between buyers and suppliers is the most cost-effective method of communication. Second, Web-based contacts from buyers provide some important signals to the supplier about the buyer's relationship orientation. In addition, participation in electronic markets (or use of Web-based initiatives) improves transaction effectiveness and efficiency. Efficiency of communication and transactions among channel members is associated with a relational structure and higher customer involvement. The important question is, How do we address this common business problem? We need to define typical objectives to understand this common business problem, which are discussed in the following section.

Typical Objectives of the Study

The Convergys example demonstrates the role of strengthening relationships in developing new and existing customers to their fullest potential, thus unlocking higher levels of profitability and ensuring client loyalty. The task is not easy, and it requires a comprehensive examination of marketing resource allocation that focuses on three questions: (1) What is the right metric for allocating resources? (2) How much do we allocate between customer acquisition and customer retention? and (3) How do we identify the resource allocation rules across various communication channels for each individual customer or customer segments?

As we go further in this study, one scenario shows how much to allocate between acquisition and retention, and another shows how much to allocate through different channels of communication. Figure 4.8 shows the key steps to follow in the allocation of resources. Let us illustrate the development of a solution to this common business through a case study.

Data Availability

The company in this case study is a large, multinational, B2B, high-technology manufacturer. The product categories in the database represent different spectra among high-technology products. Although the products are durable goods, they require constant maintenance and frequent upgrades; this characteristic provides the variance required to model the customer response. The choice of vendors for the products is normally made after much deliberation by the buyer. For the product categories, the buyer and seller choose whether to develop their relationships, and there are significant benefits to maintaining a long-standing relationship for both buyers and sellers.

The data used in the study cover a four-year period from the beginning of 1998 to the end of 2001. All the customers were new to the manufacturer, having made their first purchase in the first quarter of 1998. A total of 12,024 prospects were contacted for potential acquisition; of those, 2908 made at least one purchase in the first quarter of 1998. The average interpurchase time for an individual customer ranged between 1.5 and 21 months.

The results from our analyses show that marketing communications across various channels influence CLV in a nonlinear manner. In addition, there is the potential for substantial improvements in profits when managers design resource allocation rules that maximize CLV.

For many years, companies did not focus on the importance of CLV and the impact it had on their revenues and profitability. Typically, companies would attempt to increase revenue by continuously acquiring new customers and ignoring the ones they had in the fold. Traditional metrics used for resource allocation in support of this strategy were recency, frequency, and monetary value (RFM), share of wallet (SOW), and past customer value (PCV). These methods, how-

Figure 4.8 ♦ Allocation of Resources

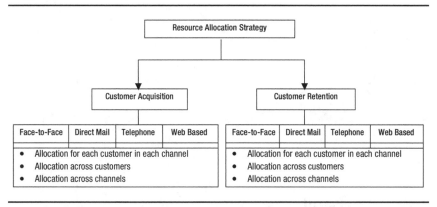

ever, are backward looking and do not consider whether a customer will be active in the future. They also consider only observed purchase behavior and assume that the future is the same as the past for each customer, and they do not incorporate the expected cost of maintaining the customer relationship in the future.

In contrast, CLV incorporates both the probability of a customer being active in the future and the marketing costs to be spent to retain the customer. Figure 4.9 offers an example of two customers, each of which generates comparable profits for the manufacturer until the 20th month. After that, Customer 1 maintains its current profitability level, whereas Customer 2 becomes increasingly less profitable. At this point, the manufacturer would greatly benefit from using a forward-looking metric to assess both customers. If a company assumes that customers will continue their past purchase behavior, managers will continue to allocate equal resources to both Customers 1 and 2. Customer 2, however, is clearly not worth pursuing. If the firm can make an accurate prediction on the purchase behavior of its customers, it can target its profitable customers with promotions and messages. Using a forward-looking metric such as CLV will save the company from incurring such losses by helping managers invest their marketing resources more wisely, thus ensuring a larger ROI for each marketing campaign (Reinartz, Thomas, and Kumar 2005).

There are several factors that, for our purposes, are important to the measurement of CLV. The key is that the measure must be forward looking because traditional metrics do not provide companies with a true measure of customer loyalty, as they assume that loyal customers are more profitable for the firm. This may be true in a con-

Figure 4.9 ♦ When Should a Firm Lose a Customer?

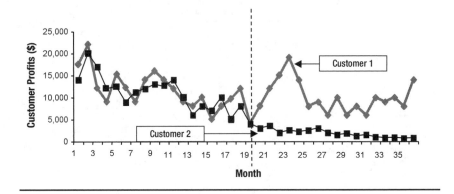

tractual setting, but in a noncontractual setting, predicting the life-time duration of a customer by observing buying patterns and other explanatory factors assumes greater importance. The poor correlation between loyalty and profitability that traditional metrics exhibit creates the need for firms to use a customer value metric such as CLV to ensure that valuable customers are and will continue to be profitable customers. The computation can also be used to include prospects, not just current customers.

Study Approach

Objective Function: CLV

The various components of CLV include purchase frequency, contribution margin, and marketing costs. In its basic form, CLV is a function of a customer's future contribution margin (e.g., marketing communications) and the propensity for a customer to continue in a relationship (customer retention). The marketing resources allocated to the customer can be calculated as follows:

$$(2) \qquad CLV_i = \sum_{t=1}^{T} \frac{(\text{Future contribution margin}_{it} - \text{Future cost}_{it})}{(1 + d)^t},$$

where i = customer index, t = time index, T = the number of time periods considered for estimating CLV, and d = discount rate.

We understand the behavior of a B2B customer in two kinds of settings: contractual and noncontractual. In a contractual setting, managers are interested in predicting customer retention or the likelihood of a customer staying in or terminating a relationship. In a noncontractual setting, the focus is more on predicting future customer activity because there is always a chance that the customer will purchase in the future. As discussed previously, a goal of calculating the value of a customer is to design customer-level strategies so that companies can maximize their return.

Is CLV a Better Metric?

The only metric that incorporates all elements of revenue, expense, and customer behavior that drives profitability is CLV. The metric also manages to score over other metrics by adopting a customer-centric approach rather than a product-centric one as the driver of profitability.

Traditionally, firms rank-order customers according to their profits and prioritize their resources on the basis of this ranking. As described previously, companies have used several customer-selection metrics such as RFM, SOW, PCV, and CLV for this purpose. Of these metrics, the forward-looking CLV metric is the most successful in predicting future customer profits.

The performance of traditional metrics versus the CLV metric in customer selection has been compared many times, with CLV consistently offering higher levels of profitability (Reinartz, Thomas, and Kumar 2005). For example, in a recent study, customers from a large high-technology services company were rank ordered from best to worst according to each metric. The total revenue, costs, and profits from the top 15% of the customers were compared over a six-year period. The net value generated by the customers who were selected according to CLV score was approximately 45% greater than that generated from customers selected through other traditional metrics. The findings show that using CLV to select customers can be far more effective than using traditional metrics, which provides substantial support for the usefulness of CLV as a metric for customer scoring and customer selection.

Allocation Decisions on Acquisition Versus Retention

Typically, firms go after customers who are easy (low cost) to acquire because they believe that the highest acquisition rate possible is ideal. In addition, acquisition and retention departments tend to act in isolation and therefore have trouble calculating profit contribution from low acquisition costs versus low retention costs. What every firm needs to understand is that, even though acquisition and retention rates may both increase, profits do not always follow suit. After a certain point, the cost of acquiring an additional customer outweighs the future stream of profits that the acquired customer will bring to the firm.

How does a firm find a balance among acquisition rate, retention rate, and overall customer profitability? To get a fairly straightforward answer to this question, we look to a marketing study by Robert Blattberg and John Deighton (1996) that examined a potential solution to the problem of balancing acquisition rates and retention rates with customer value. They asked managers how much they spent in the last year to acquire customers and how many of those customers converted from prospects to buyers. They asked managers how much was spent in the previous year to retain each customer and the percentage of customers that were still with the company. From responses to the questions, the authors were able to derive the optimal level of spending on acquisition and retention for that particular firm (see Figure 4.10).

These results show that the firm can maximize its profitability by having the right acquisition rate (near 25%) and retention rate (near 50%). These rates vary from firm to firm, but the purpose of the study is clear: At some point in time, increasing acquisition or retention rates leads to a diminishing level of overall profitability because it becomes more difficult (i.e., more expensive) to acquire or retain the next customer. Firms should invest in acquisition or retention programs only if they understand that the cost of doing so is less than the value the customer will bring back to the firm in value. Many firms have already begun to realize this and have taken steps to reward profitable managers, not the ones who maximize metrics such as acquisition and retention rates.

This can create other challenges, however, as managers focus more on short-term customer profitability (in other words, the next customer transaction) than on long-term value. This approach usually leads them to focus on customers who are easy to acquire or easy to retain, to obtain the most customers at the lowest overall cost. This approach is flawed, however, because it assumes that acquisition and retention costs are the major driver of customer profitability (see Figure 4.11).

To analyze the relationship among acquisition costs, retention costs, and customer profitability, a marketing study with a catalog retailer was undertaken (Thomas, Reinartz, and Kumar 2004). As expected, the largest segment of the group comes from the customers who are easiest to acquire and easiest to retain (i.e., casual customers). However, this group only contributed 20% of overall profitability of the entire group, with a profit-to-customer ratio of .62. The

Figure 4.10 ♦ Acquisition and Retention Rates Versus Customer Value

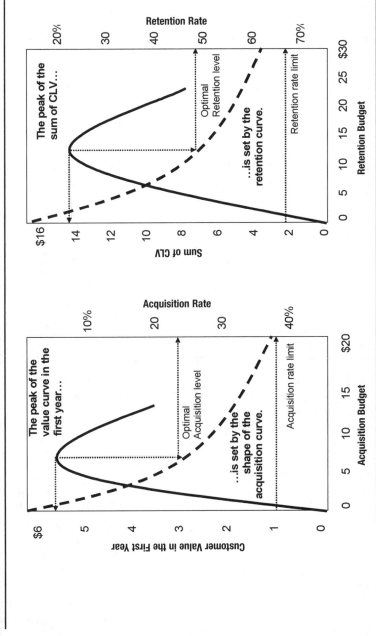

Figure 4.11 ♦ Do Acquisition and Retention Costs Drive Profits?

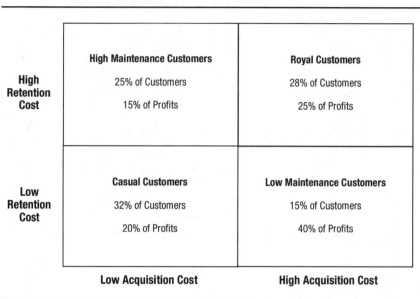

	Low Acquisition Cost	High Acquisition Cost
High Retention Cost	**High Maintenance Customers** 25% of Customers 15% of Profits	**Royal Customers** 28% of Customers 25% of Profits
Low Retention Cost	**Casual Customers** 32% of Customers 20% of Profits	**Low Maintenance Customers** 15% of Customers 40% of Profits

customers who were difficult to acquire but fairly easy to retain (i.e., low-maintenance customers) contributed the most to the profitability of this cohort (40%) but made up only 15% of total customers, for a profit-to-customer ratio of 2.67. Even the group of customers who were difficult to acquire and to retain (i.e., royal customers) contributed more in profits (25%) while numbering less than casual customers (28%), with a profit-to-customer ratio of .89.

These results are not unique to catalog firms; companies in other industries are seeing similar breakdowns of how acquisition and retention costs drive profits. Unfortunately, many companies still have suboptimal acquisition and retention practices in place.

Acquisition departments tasked with acquiring the most customers possible inevitably attract customers who are unprofitable in the long run and ignore customers that are more difficult to acquire but may be highly profitable (e.g., royal and low-maintenance customers). Retention departments whose sole focus is to retain as many customers as possible spend much of their time (and budget) on customers who are not very profitable in the long run.

For example, many credit card companies spend a lot of money on acquisition programs. Their acquisition departments use frequent direct-mail campaigns, telemarketing, and on-site promotions at airports and college campuses to lure as many customers as possible without thinking about how they will retain many of these customers as profitable. After the new customers come on board, retention departments spend a significant amount of resources trying to retain them, again devoting significant resources on customers who will never be profitable.

What can be learned from this example? Companies should consider integrating their acquisition and retention departments, which will enable them to take a long-term view of customer value and make better decisions about allocating resources to target customers and prospects that are potentially the most profitable. It is essential to understand whether it is more critical to focus on acquisition or retention expenditures when considering customer profitability and whether acquisition and retention rates are maximized at the same point as customer profitability. These questions include how a firm should allocate resources across different modes of contact (e.g., face-to-face, telephone, e-mail) because different contact modes offer different levels of interpersonal interaction.

Linking acquisition and retention to profitability is a key contribution of the CLV metric. Historically, for every $100 a company spends on advertising products and services, it dedicates more than $80 to acquiring new customers, by convincing prospects either to try its products or services for the first time or to switch back from a competitor's product. That leaves less than $20 for campaigns focused on retaining existing customers (Osenton 2002).

To better balance resource allocation between acquisition and retention initiatives, companies need to adopt a framework that can reveal the true relationships among acquisition, retention, and profits. A way to do this is by using a model we call "Allocating Resources for Profits" (ARPRO). The model involves complex regression analysis with long-term profitability as a function of several key factors and factors that are weighted and corrected for sample selection bias (Reinartz, Thomas, and Kumar 2005). It is important for a company to understand how it can implement the framework and the model's potential impact on the bottom line. Figure 4.12 shows the conceptual framework.

The objective of Figure 4.12 is to identify the relationship between prospects, acquired customers, relationship duration (retention), and customer profitability by analyzing how the actions of the company, customers, and competitors, along with customer characteristics, play a role in driving customer profitability. The resource allocation strategy falls into two categories: (1) offensive marketing and (2) defensive

Figure 4.12 ♦ Linking Acquisition, Retention, and Profitability: A Framework

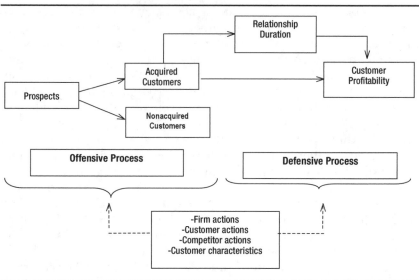

marketing. The former involves strategies designed to obtain additional customers and encourage brand switching from competition, and the latter is designed to reduce attrition and brand switching from existing customers. Resources must be allocated to both kinds of strategies simultaneously. A failure to link acquisition and retention can lead to biased results and incorrect inferences from the omission of information on nonacquired prospects.

Model and Equations

To link customer acquisition, relationship duration, and profitability, we use a system of equations known as a probit two-stage least squares model. The mathematical representations of the model are provided in Equations 5, 6, and 7.

(3) $y_{Li} = \beta'_{Ls}x_{Li} + \gamma'_{s}y_{Di} + \varepsilon_{Lis}$ if $z_i = 1$ (Cumulative profitability equation)

        $= 0$ if otherwise.

(4) $y_{Di} = \beta'_{Ds}x_{Di} + \varepsilon_{Dis}$ if $z_i = 1$ (Duration equation)

        $= 0$ if otherwise.

(5) $z_i^* = \alpha'_{s}v_i + \mu_{is}$ (Acquisition equation)

$$z_i = 1 \text{ if } z_i^* > 0$$
$$z_i = 0 \text{ if } z_i^* \leq 0,$$

where

z_i^* = a latent variable indicating customer i's utility to engage in a relationship with the firm,

z_i = an indicator variable showing whether customer i is acquired ($z_i = 1$) or not ($z_i = 0$),

v_i = a vector of covariates affecting the acquisition of customer i,

y_{Di} = the duration of customer i's relationship with the firm,

x_{Di} = a vector of covariates affecting the duration of customer i's relationship with the firm,

y_{Li} = the cumulative profitability of customer i,

x_{Li} = a vector of covariates affecting customer i's lifetime value,

$\alpha'_s, \beta'_{Ls}, \beta'_{Ds}$ = segment-specific parameters, and

$\mu_{is}, \varepsilon_{Lis}$, and ε_{Dis} = error terms.

This model determines the acquisition process, and two distinct regression equations characterize duration and long-term customer profitability. Logically, the duration and customer profitability are observed only if the customer is acquired (Reinartz, Thomas, and Kumar 2005). Thus, the duration and profitability equations are conditional regressions determined partly by the acquisition likelihood of a customer.

Profit-Maximizing ARPRO Strategy

The ultimate goal of the ARPRO framework is to develop a strategy that will maximize overall profitability in the long run. In the case of acquisition and retention, making suboptimal decisions can severely affect overall profitability. For example, given the drivers and weights of the drivers computed for this firm, the optimal average acquisition spending across customers should be $10 and the optimal average retention spending across customers should be $60 as shown in Table 4.4 (Thomas, Reinartz, and Kumar 2004).

This optimal spending on acquisition and retention provides the highest overall customer profitability for the firm. Although the difference between the levels of profitability seems small—approximately a 1.2% decrease in profitability for about a 10% savings in costs—the loss

Table 4.4 ♦ Average Customer Profitability

		Retention Spending				
		$40	$50	$60	$70	$80
Acquisition Spending	$1	$1,423	$1,543	$1,583	$1,543	$1,423
	$5	$1,437	$1,557	$1,597	$1,557	$1,437
	$10	$1,443	$1,563	$1,603	$1,563	$1,443
	$15	$1,437	$1,557	$1,597	$1,557	$1,437
	$20	$1,418	$1,538	$1,578	$1,538	$1,418

in profit grows quickly when the number of customers in the sample grows. For example, if a company cuts its marketing cost by 10% and the savings in cost is approximately $250,000, the reduction in profit is about 1.2%. This means that if the base of customers is approximately 60,000, the loss in long-term profits would be about $1.2 million. This clearly shows that when firms choose suboptimal amounts to spend on acquisition and retention, the impact on profits can be drastic.

It is also clear that acquisition and retention spending should not be done in isolation. For example, if the same firm tried to maximize only relationship duration (retention), the optimum spending level would be $70 per customer. However, the previous example shows that the optimum spending was actually $70 on both acquisition and retention—$10 on acquisition and $60 on retention per customer. By optimizing the relationship duration by spending $70 rather than splitting the $70 on acquisition ($10) and retention ($60), profitability would decrease from $1,603 to about $1,543, for a drop of 3.7% (Thomas, Reinartz, and Kumar 2004; for values, see Table 4.5). This shows that while spending too much on marketing can be detrimental to profits, spending too little can be equally or more costly.

Which Is More Critical: Acquisition or Retention Spending?

The differences in the impact of acquisition and retention spending on profitability make it difficult to decide how much to invest in each customer. This critical question arises often in marketing when budgets are constrained and decisions must be made about whether to cut acquisition spending or retention spending. For example, if the firm in this study must cut its marketing budget by 5%, should it simply reduce its acquisition and retention budgets equally? In this case, for every $1 underinvested in acquisition and retention spending, profitability was reduced by $1.25. However, what if the company focused

Table 4.5 ◆ Average Customer Relationship Duration

Retention Spending (per Customer)	$40	$50	$60	$70	$80
Estimated Relationship Duration (Days)	122	135	142	143	138

its budget cut by reducing acquisition costs only? In this case, for every $1 decrease in spending, the resulting decrease in long-term profitability would be $3.03.

In this case, an equal decrease in spending for acquisition and retention would result in a higher long-term customer profit. These results can be influenced by many different factors, so it is necessary for companies to perform their own analysis of how deviations in spending affect overall profitability.

How Much to Allocate Across Communication Channels to Retain Customers?

To develop and implement customized marketing strategies, it is essential for companies to understand the exact nature of the various links (e.g., strength, symmetry, nonlinearity) for efficient allocation of resources. The importance of CLV is that because it is forward looking, it can help marketers adopt appropriate marketing activities today to increase future profitability. The computation can also be used to include prospects, not just current customers.

Some recent studies provide a few examples on optimizing resources to maximize CLV (e.g., Thomas, Reinartz, and Kumar 2004). It is necessary to keep in mind that the firm does not necessarily achieve optimal profitability by optimizing CLV, nor are profitability and CLV positively correlated. For example, studies on a pharmaceutical company indicate that spending more than optimal values on acquisition and retention may result in a significant increase in customer profitability but a reduction in overall profitability of the firm. This shows that the optimal balance between investments in acquisition and retention can be more important than finding the optimum amount to invest overall.

Marketing communication decisions can be addressed by considering the following (Galper 1979):

◆ The size of the total communications budget for a product;

◆ Decisions on the mix of communications elements, particularly personal selling and advertising; and

◆ Expenditure decisions for individual communications elements.

Objective Function: CLV Model

A more advanced model by Venkatesan and Kumar (2004) for calculating CLV focuses on the interpurchase time (quantified by frequency), which they modeled by fitting a distribution over the past interpurchase behavior of the customer and by taking the expectation value of this distribution. Use of frequency accounts for customers who are dormant for a particular period of time (as frequently occurs in customer purchases such as automobiles or computers) and who then come back to the firm. This provides a more realistic and robust prediction of the purchase behavior of customers. Therefore, the lifetime value of a customer can be calculated as follows:

$$(6) \quad CLV_{it} = \underbrace{\sum_{t=1}^{T_i} \frac{GC_{i,t}}{(1+r)^t / frequency_i}}_{\text{PV of gross contribution}} - \underbrace{\sum_{l=1}^{n} \frac{\sum_m c_{i,m,l} \times x_{i,m,l}}{(1+r)^l}}_{\text{PV of marketing cost}}$$

where

CLV = customer lifetime value,

$GC_{i,t}$ = gross contribution from customer i in purchase occasion t,

$c_{i,m,l}$ = unit marketing cost for customer i in channel m in year l,

$x_{i,m,l}$ = number of contacts to customer i in channel m in year l,

$frequency_i$ = 12/$expint_i$ (where $expint_i$ = expected interpurchase time for customer i),

r = the discount rate for money,

n = number of years to forecast, and

T_i = number of purchases made by distributor i, until the end of the planning period.

We predict the contribution from a customer in each purchase occasion over the next three years, the number of marketing contacts, and the marketing costs in different channels using the following information: Various supplier-specific factors (channel communication) and customer characteristics (involvement, switching costs, and previous behavior) are identified as the antecedents of purchase frequency and contribution margin. The purchase frequency and contribution margin are then related to the antecedents using sophisticated models. The future marketing costs are also predicted using information from the past marketing activities and the response to those activities. The CLV model described previously can be employed to identify the responsiveness of customers to marketing communication through different channels of communication, which is the basis for optimal allocation of marketing resources across channels of contact for each customer so as to maximize his or her respective CLV.

In addition to using the CLV framework for a resource allocation strategy, it can be used for formulating other customer-level strategies, such as customer selection and purchase sequence analysis, and for targeting right customers for acquisition. The measurement of CLV for each customer enables managers to optimally allocate resources so that CLV can be maximized.

In the preceding model, $x_{i,m,l}$ gives the number of customer contacts made in a particular channel in a given period. This includes in-person contacts initiated by the sales team and direct-mail and telephone contacts. The marketing costs incurred in such contacts is given by $c_{i,m,l}$. The frequency factor (frequency$_i$) helps in forecasting the purchase frequency in the following years. The term $GC_{i,t}$ predicts the gross contribution margin made by a customer in each future purchase occasion. Similarly, future marketing cost ($MC_{i,l,m}$) is also generated for each customer.

Optimal Resource Allocation Strategy

Applying this strategy to the B2B technology firm demonstrates its efficacy. Traditionally, the company had categorized customers according to their SOW. In implementing the CLV-based framework, customers were segmented into four sections based on their SOW and CLV (Thomas, Reinartz, and Kumar 2004). For each segment, detailed recommendations were made regarding the optimal number of face-to-face meetings, direct-mail contacts, telesales, and so on. The results of these recommendations are summarized in Figure 4.13. Here, the original level of profitability and marketing spending of each segment is given along with the results generated by switching to an optimal allocation strategy.

As the results show, the B2B firm was consistently overspending on the low-CLV customers (Cells 3 and 4 in Figure 4.13). This is a classic example of how firms pursue low-value customers and spend valuable marketing resources on them. Particularly, the firm was using the expensive face-to-face channel of contact frequently, thus increasing marketing spending dramatically. After adopting a CLV-based approach, the company reduced face-to-face contacts for customers in Cell 3 from once every 5 months to once every 13 months (a similar measure was adopted for customers in Cell 4). By cutting spending levels in half, profits for this segment increased by more than 200%.

Figure 4.13 ◆ Optimal Resource Allocation Strategy Applied for a B2B Technology Firm

	Low SOW	High SOW
High CLV	Cost Reduction ($): **Cell 1** Current Spending: $1,008 Optimal Spending Limit: $2,197 Face-to-Face Meetings: Current Frequency: once every 7 months Optimal Frequency: once every 5 months Direct Mail/Telesales: Current Interval: 6 days Optimal Interval: 2 days Profits: Current Profit: $109,364 Optimal profit: $178,092	Cost Reduction ($): **Cell 2** Currently Spending: $1,385 Optimal Spending Limit: $2,419 Face-to-Face Meetings: Current Frequency: once every 3 months Optimal Frequency: once every 1 month Direct Mail/Telesales: Current Interval: 6 days Optimal Interval: 5 days Profits: Current Profit is $534,888 Optimal profit is $905,224
Low CLV	Cost Reduction ($): **Cell 3** Currently Spending: $819 Optimal Spending Limit: $433 Face-to-Face Meetings: Current Frequency: once every 5 months Optimal Frequency: once every 13 months Direct Mail/Telesales: Current Interval: 10 days Optimal Interval: 13 days Profits: Current Profit: $7,435 Optimal profit: $12,030	Cost Reduction ($): **Cell 4** Currently Spending: $1,291 Optimal Spending Limit: $612 Face-to-Face Meetings: Current Frequency: once every 2 months Optimal Frequency: once every 10 months Direct Mail/Telesales: Current Interval: 8 days Optimal Interval: 8 days Profits: Current Profit: $10,913 Optimal profit: $28,354

At the same time, the firm was consistently underspending on the high-CLV customers (as represented in Cells 1 and 2), which prevented it from fully exploiting the profit potential of the group. Under its CLV-based approach, the company nearly doubled the marketing spending on high-value customers by contacting them more frequently (using both face-to-face contacts and direct mail/telesales), which resulted in a significant increase in profits.

By carefully monitoring the purchase frequency of customers, the interpurchase time, and the contribution to profits, managers could determine the frequency of marketing initiatives to maximize CLV. Across all four cells, using the CLV-based strategy to reallocate marketing resources helped the company double revenues and increase profits by 70%.

Challenges in Implementation

The implementation of CLV strategies poses challenges to B2B companies. Many firms do not use CLV measurements judiciously. A main reason for the failure of the strategies is that companies do not support the effort fully or do not customize and execute the implementation across departments. Another challenge is for firms to collect the right data. In particular, organizations that sell through intermediaries find it difficult (if not impossible) to gather data about end customers with whom they have no direct contact. A sound CLV-based strategy requires data collection efforts focused on four main characteristics:

1. Data should be at the customer level.

2. Data should contain all transaction information, including past customer value, recency, frequency, and contribution margin to derive profitability drivers.

3. The longer the span of data collection, the better are the data. At minimum, companies should collect data for a two- to three-year period.

4. Data should comprise all marketing touch methods used (e.g., mail, e-mail) and the date each touch occurred.

After collecting data with these characteristics, marketing managers can develop a customer-level strategy to aid decision making. In business environments in which decisions about allocating marketing resources increasingly occur at the individual account level, it is critical for marketers to understand that individuals who are easy to acquire and retain may not be the most profitable customers. The resource allocation choices will provide a clear set of attainable, profit-linked marketing goals for which managers can be held accountable.

Key Learnings

Several key learnings have been gained from the study conducted. First, both acquisition and retention spending are critical because for every $1 underinvested in acquisition and retention spending, profitability was reduced by $1.25. Equal decreases in spending for acquisition and retention would result in a higher long-term customer profit. Second, integrating a company's acquisition and retention departments enables the groups to take a better long-term view of customer profitability rather than work independently to acquire and retain as many customers as possible—even those who may not be profitable. Third, channels are classified according to modes of communications and type of customers. Finally, companies should allocate resources across channels and customers to maximize CLV, rather than focusing on backward-looking metrics such as share of wallet or past customer value.

◆ CONCLUSION

The ability to know when, what, and how many resources to allocate across communications channels will help marketing managers invest in the most profitable customers at the most appropriate time and in the most effective way, which in turn can increase revenue and profit gained from them. Rather than spending valuable resources on large numbers of unprofitable customers, companies should adopt a customer value framework that enables them to allocate resources optimally to focus on the customers and prospects that hold the potential to create the most long-term value.

The previous case studies provide evidence that optimal allocation of marketing resources among marketing mix variables helps companies increase their revenue, balance acquisition and retention of customers, and manage customers profitably.

◆ NOTES

1. Because heuristics for new media were not available, Company A decided to experiment with different formats such as pop-up alerts, Web presence, and e-mail marketing. As time-series data on new media become available, the resource optimization models can integrate those new media options.

◆ REFERENCES

Bachman, Katy (2007), "Nielsen: Ad Spend Rises 4.6% in '06," (March 19), (accessed March 2, 2008), [available at http://www.mediaweek.com/mw/news/recent_display.jsp?vnu_content_id=1003560033].

Berger, Paul D. and Nada I. Nasr (1998), "Customer Lifetime Value: Marketing Models and Applications," *Journal of Interactive Marketing*, 12 (1), 17–30.

Blattberg, Robert C. and John Deighton (1996), "Manage Marketing by the Customer Equity Test," *Harvard Business Review*, 74 (4), 136–44.

Galper, Morton (1979), "Communications Spending Decisions for Industrial Products: A Literature Review," (accessed February 18, 2008), [available at http://www.msi.org/publications/publication.cfm?pub=100].

IBM Consumer Study (2007), "Internet Rivals Declining TV as Primary Media Source," (accessed September 11, 2007), [available at http://www.marketingcharts.com/television/ibm-consumer-study-internet-rivals-declining-tv-as-primary-media-source-1340/].

Interactive Advertising Bureau (2003), "The Cross Media Optimization Study (XMOS)," (accessed November 27, 2007), [available at http://www.iab.net/insights_research/iab_research/1672/1678/1690].

Osenton, Tom (2002), "Customer Share Marketing: Getting the Most Out of Your Customers," (accessed September 11, 2007), [available at http://www.phptr.com/articles/printerfriendly.asp?p=26653].

Peppers, D. and M. Rogers (1993), *The One to One Future: Building Relationships One Customer at a Time.* New York: Currency/Doubleday.

Reinartz, Werner, Jacquelyn S. Thomas, and V. Kumar (2005), "Balancing Acquisition and Retention Resources to Maximize Customer Profitability," *Journal of Marketing,* 69 (January), 63–79.

Thomas, Jacquelyn S., Werner Reinartz, and V. Kumar (2004), "Getting the Most Out of All Your Customers," *Harvard Business Review,* 82 (7–8), 116–23.

Venkatesan, R. and V. Kumar (2004), "A Customer Lifetime Value Framework for Customer Selections and Resource Allocation Strategy," *Journal of Marketing,* 68 (October), 106–125.

CHAPTER 5

STRATEGIC ALLOCATION OF MARKETING RESOURCES: METHODS AND INSIGHTS

Venkatesh Shankar, Texas A&M University

◆ INTRODUCTION AND OVERVIEW OF RESOURCE ALLOCATION

Marketing resource allocation is a strategic priority for organizations worldwide. From the largest enterprise to the smallest start-up, marketing resource allocation continues to dominate the decision-making realm of the chief marketing officer (CMO) and other marketing executives. Many marketers live and die by the marketing allocation strategies they help formulate and execute. According to a recent CMO Council (2007) report, the number-one challenge for most CMOs is to quantify, measure, and improve the value of marketing investments and resource allocation. Therefore, a deep understanding of marketing resource allocation is critical for practitioners and academics alike.

Marketing executives are interested in marketing resource allocation methods and the associated substantive insights they can apply in practice. The key marketing resource allocation decisions include those between marketing and product-related variables such as

The author thanks Jeff Meyer for data collection assistance and Gary Lilien, Roger Kerin, Tarun Kushwaha, and an AMA reviewer for helpful comments.

research and development (R&D); across different products and brands, marketing mix elements, markets, countries, customers, and channels; and over the product life cycle. An overview of these types of decisions appears in Figure 5.1. To assist these decisions, marketing researchers have developed several resource allocation models. The applications of these models have led to several useful empirical findings and insights.

Consider the marketing resource allocation problem at Samsung Electronics, one of the world's leading electronics companies. In 1999, Eric Kim, at the time Samsung's new executive vice president and CMO, was challenged to reallocate a corporate budget of $1 billion across 14 products over 200 countries and to improve the return on marketing spending.[1] Before the reallocation exercise, the company had allocated resources to products and countries roughly in proportion to the sizes of the products and markets. Faced with the reallocation task, Samsung collected data on variables such as country population, population of target buyers, spending power per capita, per capita spending on product category, category penetration rate, category growth, category profitability, share of the company's brand, media costs, previous marketing expenditures, and competitor actions. Samsung developed a resource allocation model based on these factors and simulated forecasts of future profits based on the revised model.

How did the new model change resource allocation at Samsung? It informed Samsung that the company had invested more in North America and Russia than the profit potentials in those regions justified. Following this analysis, Samsung reduced the total shares of the budget to these regions from 45% to 35%. Furthermore, the model pointed out that the firm had underinvested in Europe and China, so Samsung increased the combined shares of the budget for those regions from 31% to 42%.

With regard to products, the model suggested that three categories—mobile phones, vacuum cleaners, and air-conditioning units—were getting more than half the marketing budget, but other potentially profitable categories (i.e., camcorders, DVD players and recorders, televisions, PC monitors, refrigerators, and VCRs) were being starved of support. This finding convinced Samsung to reduce its spending on mobile phones, vacuum cleaners, and air-conditioning units by 22%.

What were the results of the resource reallocation in Samsung? In 2002, the company achieved significant market share gains in four categories in which it increased marketing spend: camcorders, flat-panel computer monitors, DVD players and recorders, and digital televisions. It catapulted from tenth to third in the digital music player

Figure 5.1 ◆ An Overview of the Types of Resource Allocation Decisions

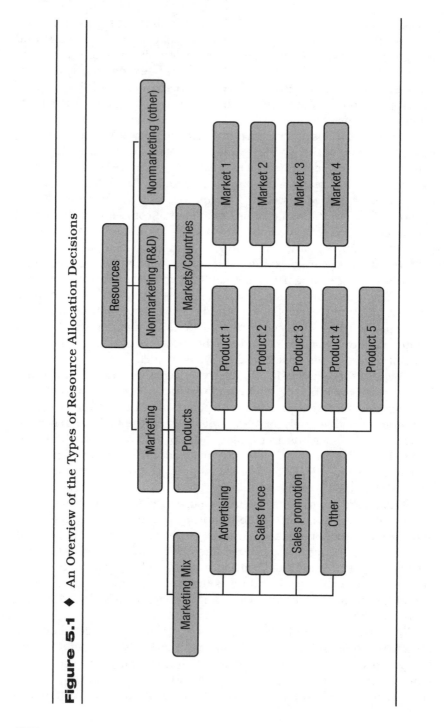

market, from eighth to second in the LCD monitor market, and from an insignificant rank to eighth in the portable DVD player market. Furthermore, Samsung's brand value increased by 30% to $8.3 billion, while the brand value of its closest rival, Sony, decreased by 7% to $13.9 billion during the same period. Samsung's annual sales rose 25% from $27.7 billion in 2001 to $34.7 billion in 2002, while its net income grew from $5.1 billion in 2001 to $5.9 billion in 2002. These improved results could be attributed at least in part to marketing resource reallocation. As Samsung's resource reallocation experience suggests, effective allocation of resources can help spiral a company's performance and brand value upward.

Types and Principles of Resource Allocation Models

Regardless of the allocation context, normative models of resource allocation can be classified into four broad types: (1) a set of optimization rules applied to an econometrically estimated model, (2) empirical models that offer norms for strategic decision making, (3) analytical models with or without empirical estimation of market-specific parameters, and (4) decision calculus models in which the parameters are assessed by managerial input (Gatignon 1993). The first two types of models are quite similar in approach. Herein, we primarily review the first three types of models. For more on decision calculus models (e.g., Little 1970; Lodish 1971), see Chapter 1.[2]

In all the types of models, optimal resource allocation is based on the fundamental microeconomic and mathematical principle that an optimal level of spending on an element of resource allocation is that at which the marginal return from an investment in that element equals the marginal costs of that investment. Many resource allocation decisions are based on elasticities or responsiveness and costs or margins associated with the variables involved in the allocation problem. Elasticity of a variable is the percentage change in the outcome variable (sales or profits) in response to a percentage change in that variable. A key decision rule is to allocate most resources to the variable with the highest elasticity.

◆ STRATEGIC ALLOCATION OF MARKETING AND PRODUCT-RELATED RESOURCES

Whether at the corporate, business unit, or product line level, executives frequently make decisions on allocating resources to both marketing activities and nonmarketing activities, such as R&D. Although firms base such decisions on factors such as past decisions, the type of industry, whether the product is new or existing, market responsiveness, and the interrelation among the different variables, not much is known about the effectiveness of such decisions. Furthermore, there is a dearth of tools for such resource allocation decisions.

Allocation Between R&D and Marketing

Allocation between R&D and marketing is a strategic decision. Consider, for example, the pharmaceutical industry. In 2006, pharmaceutical companies in North America spent roughly $55.2 billion on R&D, or 19.4% of sales (PhRMA 2007), and $27.3 billion on marketing expenditures, or approximately 10% of sales, for a total outlay of $83 billion, or approximately 30% of revenues, against industry sales of $274.9 billion. With such a large outlay on R&D and marketing, allocating resources between them has critical implications for the returns to the firm.

The development of models for allocating resources between R&D and marketing has been a subject of discussion and debate among academics and practitioners. Any effective model for allocation between these two (or more) strategic variables involves a deep understanding of the industry, the competitive context, the unique effects of each variable on firm profits, and the effects of interactions among the variables.

Two issues make the formulation of an allocation model for R&D and marketing challenging. First, although marketing expenditures have both short-term and long-term effects on firm sales and profits (Dekimpe and Hanssens 1999), R&D investments primarily have a long-term effect on firm profits (Erickson and Jacobson 1992). Second, the interactions between R&D and marketing investments and their impact on firm profits are complex. On the one hand, higher marketing expenditures can enhance the effectiveness of R&D spending, leading to increased R&D levels. On the other hand, greater marketing spending can lead to lower R&D spending, given that most firms have fixed resources.

Most models do not deal directly with this high level of strategic allocation. There are, however, descriptive models that study the effects of R&D and marketing variables on returns and profits (e.g., Bayus, Erickson, and Jacobson 2003; Erikson and Jacobson 1992) and offer implications for resource allocation between these variables. Erickson and Jacobson (1992) estimate an econometric model of the effects of R&D and advertising expenditures on stock market returns and return on investment and conclude that after controlling for unobservable firm-specific factors and the feedback between discretionary expenditures and profitability, the accounting and stock market returns to R&D and advertising expenditures are substantially lower than previously believed. These findings imply that companies should not allocate more expenditures to either R&D or marketing than required. Bayus, Erickson, and Jacobson (2003) analyze financial returns from new product introductions in the computer industry. They find that greater R&D spending and new product introduction is accompanied by a reduction in marketing spending and that these changes lead to higher profit rates.

In practice, however, many firms set their R&D and marketing budgets according to one of the following methods: objectives and task, percentage of sales revenues, percentage change from the previous period, or competitive parity. These methods do not address the optimality of allocation between R&D and marketing, so there is a strong need for optimal models of and insights into resource allocation between R&D and marketing expenditures.

Figures 5.2 and 5.3 capture the resource allocation trends among R&D; selling, general, and administrative (SG&A) expenses; and advertising during 2001–2005 for *Fortune* 500 companies. The firms are divided into the following categories of industries: consumer

---

Figure 5.2 ♦ Annual Advertising and R&D Expenditures for *Fortune* 500 Firms

---

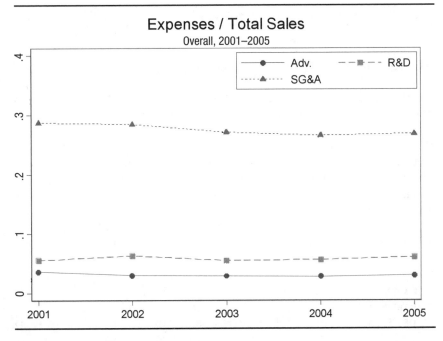

Expenses / Total Sales
Overall, 2001–2005

Figure 5.3 ♦ Annual Advertising and R&D Expenditures for *Fortune* 500 Firms by Sector

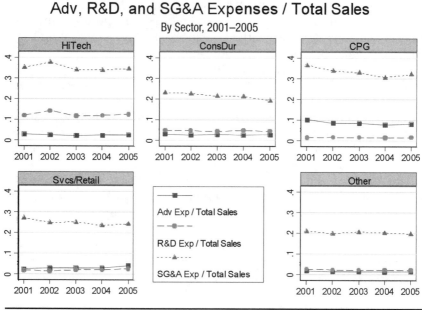

Adv, R&D, and SG&A Expenses / Total Sales
By Sector, 2001–2005

Notes: HiTech = high-technology, ConsDur = consumer durables, and Svcs/Retail = services/retail.

packaged goods (CPGs), consumer durables, services/retail, high-tech, and other.

During 2001–2005, SG&A, advertising, and R&D expenses as a percentage of sales remained fairly stable. Across industries, R&D expenses as a percentage of sales were consistently higher (2%–3%) than advertising expenses as a percentage of sales. The high-tech and CPG sectors had the highest SG&A expenses as a percentage of sales. The high-tech sector had the highest R&D expenses as a percentage of sales, while the CPG sector had the highest advertising expenses as a percentage of sales.

During 2001–2005, in the consumer durables and CPG sectors, SG&A expenses as a percentage of sales fell by approximately 4%, while advertising and R&D expenses as a percentage of sales remained fairly stable. In the services/retail sector, SG&A expenses as a percentage of sales fell by approximately 3%, while advertising and R&D expenses as a percentage of sales rose by approximately 2% and 1%, respectively. The high-tech sector consistently had the highest R&D

expenditures as a percentage of SG&A expenses, while the services/retail and CPG sectors had the lowest R&D expenditures. In the services/retail sector, both advertising and R&D expenses as a percentage of SG&A expenses rose by approximately 6% and 4%, respectively. Other than the consumer durables sector, which saw a jump of approximately 4% in 2005, all other sectors' advertising and R&D expenses as a percentage of SG&A expenses remained fairly stable.

In summary, allocation to R&D is higher for high-tech firms, while allocation to marketing is higher for consumer goods firms. During 2001–2005, expenditures on R&D and marketing remained stable for most industries except for service firms, which increased both R&D and marketing expenditures over this period. Firms should be careful not to overspend on R&D or marketing, and often, if they increase R&D expenditures, they also reduce marketing spending.

When firms decide how much of the budget to allocate to marketing, the next decision is how to spread those dollars across different marketing elements, such as advertising, sales force support, and sales promotion. Marketing mix allocation is widely practiced by many firms, though the marketing mix variables vary considerably across industries. In the pharmaceutical industry, for example, of the total industry marketing spending of $27 billion in 2006, $15.9 billion was spent on detailing and samples, $7.2 billion was expended on other professional physician marketing efforts (e.g., journal advertising), and $4.2 billion was spent on direct-to-consumer advertising (IMS Health 2006). Thus, a majority of allocation is toward sales force efforts.

In contrast, in the CPG industry, the bulk of the allocation is divided between advertising and sales promotion. For example, Procter & Gamble used a marketing mix model to move approximately $400 million of its 2005 marketing budget of $4.3 billion to advertising in new media, and Clorox used a marketing mix model to shift its allocation from advertising to sales promotion (Neff 2004).

Allocation Between Advertising and the Sales Force

Advertising and sales force expenditures form a big chunk of firms' marketing spending in many markets, including those for industrial, high-tech, and pharmaceutical products. Lilien (1979) analyzed marketing expenditure allocation data obtained during the 1970s on 131 diversified industrial products from 22 companies through the ADVISOR, a joint project of Massachusetts Institute of Technology and the Association of National Advertisers. The findings from Lilien's analysis show that firms' allocation toward the sales force relative to advertising depends on its size, the size of an average order, the stage in the product's life cycle, the complexity of the product, the fraction of the product's sales made-to-order, and the purchase frequency of the product.

Often, marketing mix variables, such as advertising and sales force, are correlated. Rangaswamy and Krishnamurthi (1991) propose an equity estimator for estimating regression models of sales response in which the marketing mix variables are typically multicollinear. Their application to pharmaceutical data shows that firms should spend more on the sales force than on advertising because sales force elasticities are much higher than those for advertising for ethical drugs.

Shankar (1997) develops optimal allocation rules based on a decoupled multiplicative sales response model of allocation between advertising and the sales force. The model allows for the interaction between advertising and the sales force and is specified as follows:

(1) $$S_{it} = e^{a_{it}} A_{it}^{b_i} A_{jt}^{c_i} D_{it}^{d_i} D_{jt}^{f_i} P_{it}^{-g_i} P_{jt}^{h_i}, \text{ with } a_{it} = \alpha_i - \frac{\phi_i}{T_{it}},$$

where S_{it} is units sales, A_{it} is the advertising spending, D_{it} is the sales force spending, P_{it} is the unit price, and T_{it} is the "time in market" of brand i in period t. The terms a–h, α, and ϕ are parameters to be estimated, and j is the main competitor brand. Maximizing the profit function, Π, with respect to advertising, sales force spending, and price provides the following:

(2) $$\max_{A,D,P} \Pi_{it} = m_{it}S_{it} - A_{it} - D_{it} - F_{it},$$

where m_{it} denotes the contribution margin and F is other fixed costs. Shankar derives the following equilibrium levels of spending for advertising and the sales force, respectively:

(3) $$A_{it}^* = b_i m_{it} S_{it}, \text{ and } D_{it}^* = d_i m_{it} S_{it}.$$

This result is an extension of the Dorfman and Steiner (1954) theorem on price and advertising elasticities. This result holds (1) if both the competitors play a Nash game or make their marketing mix decisions simultaneously or (2) if the competitor is a Stackelberg follower or makes the decision after the focal brand in one or all of the marketing instruments. Shankar develops equilibrium reactions under Nash and different leader–follower games and illustrates the analytical results with an empirical analysis of data from a large pharmaceutical market.

From these results and the assumptions, Shankar explains the focal brand's marketing mix allocation on using empirical analysis of simultaneous and sequential games. He finds that the type of competitive game and the anticipated impact of the competitor on the focal brand's margin and elasticities are two critical factors that significantly affect the brand's resource allocation decisions, in addition to the brand's characteristics and the market conditions considered by prior research. The results show that, in general, a follower (leader) role in a marketing mix variable, a static (growing) market, a decrease (increase) in own elasticity, and margin all lead to a reduction of spending in that variable.

Shankar also highlights cases in which general allocation decisions don't hold and points out that it is necessary to examine not only one factor at a time but also a combination of all the factors. He argues that the shift in marketing mix allocation follows changes in its relative marketing mix effectiveness, which depends on the structure of competition, the impact of the competitor on the brand's elasticities and margins, and the competitor's marketing mix. Shankar's model and results offer compelling insights into the allocation between advertising and the sales force. The allocation strategies proposed by his model are both theoretically and empirically driven, so they have important normative implications for managers. His empirical analysis, however, is based on one product category.

Collectively, these models offer some generalizable insights into allocation between advertising and the sales force. The spending level on a marketing variable, such as advertising or sales force, is typically directly proportional to the elasticity of the variable and contribution margin. Managers should allocate spending between advertising and the sales force according to their competitively relative elasticities. These elasticities may differ across industries, markets, and firms.

Allocation Between Advertising and Sales Promotion

In many markets, marketers need to decide the levels of expenditures for advertising and sales promotion. This decision is particularly important for consumer products and services. For CPGs, during the past two decades, the spending on advertising relative to sales promotion has steadily declined. For some of these products, sales promotion now constitutes two-thirds or more of marketing spending.

Many practitioners follow several rules of thumb, including spending 75% of the budget on proven media, message, and channels and at least 5% on well-designed marketing allocation experiments. Several factors have contributed to the continuing dominance of sales promotion over advertising for CPGs. First, most consumers make purchase decisions at the point of purchase, compelling marketers to spend more on in-store features, display, and other merchandising activities. Second, retailers have become more powerful over the years, so trade promotions have increased considerably. Third, mass media advertising has become fragmented and less effective with the advent and growth of the Internet, digital video recorders, and more targeted communication vehicles.

A few studies have examined the allocation between advertising and trade promotions. Sethuraman and Tellis (1991) incorporate two facets of trade promotions (price cuts) into the Dorfman and Steiner (1954) model of allocation: the opportunity loss from buyers who would have bought at the regular price and the loss from retailers' fractional pass-through of promotions to consumers. They find that when both promotion and advertising are profitable, the allocation between them is determined by their relative elasticities. Specifically, they find that for consumer nondurable goods, price cut elasticity is approximately 20 times that of advertising elasticity, while for durable goods, the corresponding ratio is only five.

Neslin, Powell, and Stone (1995) analytically extend the substitutability of advertising and trade promotion in optimal allocation to a dynamic context that includes a retailer's forward-buying behavior and carryover effects of advertising. Such a lopsided ratio of promotion to advertising elasticities may explain the migration of marketing dollars toward sales promotion for CPGs during recent years. However, because advertising has long-term effects (Dekimpe and Hanssens 1999), companies may be myopic in overallocating to sales promotion on the basis of short-term effects.

Although there are rules of thumb and marketing mix models that guide the allocation of marketing spending between advertising and sales promotion, many of these are not based on optimization principles. A major challenge in developing optimal allocation models between advertising and sales promotion is that often these two variables have synergistic effects on sales and profits, making it difficult to disentangle their unique effects. Naik, Raman, and Winer (2005) propose a model for allocation between advertising and sales promotion when the two have interaction effects and when managers can incorporate strategic foresight about competitor behavior. They use an extended Lancaster model and develop a continuous-discrete estimation method to calibrate dynamic models of oligopoly using market data. In their optimization model, brand i decides its advertising (u) and promotional expenditures (v) to maximize its performance index, given by the following:

(4) $$I\left(u_i, v_i\right) = \int_{t=0}^{T} e^{-\rho t}\left\{\left[p_i(t) - v_i(t)\right]m_i(t) - c\left[u_i(t)\right]\right\}dt,$$

where ρ is the discount rate, p is the brand price, m is the market share, c is the cost of advertising, T is the total number of periods over which the allocation is done, and t is time. Solving this dynamic optimization model using data on five detergent brands, Naik, Raman, and Winer find that large brands underadvertise and overpromote, while small brands underadvertise and underpromote and that competitor responses to advertising and promotion are asymmetric.

In summary, consumer goods companies increasingly allocate more toward sales promotion and nontraditional media relative to advertising in the mass media, mainly because short-term mass media advertising elasticities are much smaller than elasticities of promotion or targeted media advertising. When interactions between advertising and sales promotions are included, large brands tend to underadvertise and overpromote, while small brands tend to underadvertise and underpromote.

Other Marketing Mix Allocations

Several models of marketing mix allocation across other elements exist (Mantrala 2002). Others include those on media mix, sales territory allocation (Rangaswamy, Sinha, and Zoltners 1990), direct-mail campaigns (Elsner, Krafft, and Huchzermeier 2004), and product and nonproduct marketing elements (Shankar 2006). The marketing mix involving nontraditional media is gaining ground in today's environment. According to A.G. Lafley, chief executive officer of Procter & Gamble, although the company still invests mostly in television, the media mix for major brands now includes a greater focus on in-store, Internet, and nonmeasured media (Tode 2007).

Furthermore, managers need to make allocation decisions that are simultaneously related to product line length, channel coverage, and pricing. Shankar (2006) develops a simultaneous model of demand and supply with product line and other marketing actions, which can be used to identify reaction and anticipation elasticities through the rational expectations approach. He estimates the model using data from the computer printer market, which comprises the market leader, Hewlett-Packard, and followers, Epson, Canon, and Lexmark. The results show that the market leader practices a product proliferation strategy and rarely fights on price. In contrast, market followers adopt a price-fighting strategy. A firm is more likely to allocate more to expanding a product line when its competitors changed their product lines in the past, when the firm is large, and when its price is high. Product line reaction and anticipation elasticities are asymmetric between themselves and across the firms. For the market leader (followers), product line reaction elasticity is higher (lower) than product line anticipation elasticity. These differences are related to product line demand elasticities, which are higher for the market leader than they are for the followers. For additional details on these allocation decisions, see Chapters 1 and 4.

◆ ALLOCATION ACROSS PRODUCTS

Marketers make decisions on the allocation of funds toward different products and brands in their product portfolio. Models on allocation across products range from product portfolio models to models for a specific industry context (e.g., Mantrala, Sinha, and Zoltners 1992). Among product portfolio models, the Boston Consulting Group (BCG) matrix (Henderson 1998) is the best-known tool. This matrix begins with identifying the positions of a firm's or a business unit's products along two dimensions: relative market share and market growth rate. Products can fall under four possible quadrants. (1) "Cash cows" are products that are characterized by high relative market share but low market growth rate, (2) "stars" are those that have both high growth rate and relative market share, (3) "question marks" or "problem children" refer to products that have low relative market share in high-growth markets, and (4) "dogs" are products that have low relative market share in low-growth markets. The main resource allocation guidelines are to use the surplus cash from "cash cows" and "stars" (if any) to fund "question marks" so as to help them become "stars" for the future and to divest "dogs" unless they are strategic complements to other products or have substantial exit barriers.

Many firms practice variants of this tool (Kerin, Mahajan, and Varadarajan 1990). The enhancements to the BCG model are based on the recognition that relative market share is a proxy for competitive strength, and market growth is a measure of market attractiveness. For example, General Electric uses a model that has these two broad dimensions, which are determined by multiple indicators that include relative market share and market growth.

Despite their widespread use, product portfolio models suffer from several limitations. First, they do not explicitly incorporate profits or margins as a major criterion. They implicitly assume that profits are correlated with relative market share. Second, the allocation rules from these models are based on a static view of the business universe. In reality, fast movement in markets and competitive dynamics may alter some product positions in the matrix, calling for changes in allocation rules that are difficult to make after investments are made on analysis of the original matrix. Third, the definitions of high- and low-growth rates or relative market shares are subjective, driving the categorization of products as "stars," "question marks," "cash cows," or "dogs" and the allocation rules. Therefore, although the portfolio models provide a useful high-level basis for resource allocation across products, they should be supplemented with more granular resource allocation models that are more detailed and specific to the industry and the firm.

Richardson (2004) develops and applies a linear programming model to allocate marketing funds for Reckitt and Coleman's (now Reckitt and Benckiser's) products, including Lysol. His approach involves weighing several company-specific criteria, such as market growth, brand share, brand sales, contribution, and market size, against the budget constraints of the project, group, business unit, and firm levels. He claims that the model led to improved profits, simultaneous examination of alternatives, fast response to unexpected situations, and better utilization of the data at the firm.

Taken together, models and studies of allocation across products offer interesting insights. Firms should use the profits generated by "cash cows" to allocate more funds toward products with greater future potential. In deciding which products have greater future potential, firms should use multiple factors that reflect the attractiveness of the markets and the firm's competitive position.

◆ ALLOCATION ACROSS MARKETS AND COUNTRIES

Allocation across different markets or countries is an important but challenging task. It requires a deep understanding of the response behavior of customers in different regions. Differences in responses across markets and countries increase the complexity of decision making. As previously noted in the Samsung example, however, resource allocation based on a careful analysis of the factors that drive the differences across countries can result in substantial improvements in allocation decisions. These market- or country-specific factors include the population of target buyers, spending power per capita, per capita spending on product category, category penetration rate, category growth, category profitability, share of the company's brand, media costs, previous marketing expenditures, and competitor actions.

Lilien and Rao (1976) propose a model for allocating retail outlet building resources across different markets for a consumer product. They maximize the net present value of expected returns from a construction plan that comprises several different outlets in different markets subject to size constraints, and they determine the optimal plan. The model is based on an S-shaped relationship between outlet share and market share. Lilien and Rao implemented their model in a consumer goods firm in which the model went on to become an integral part of the planning process.

In addition to market-specific factors, some cross-market factors such as diffusion, market learning, and multimarket competition may drive allocation rules. Chintagunta and Desiraju (2005) develop a structural model that incorporates both cross-market contact effects, in addition to interaction effects, across marketing instruments and within-market competitive interaction effects, consistent with the theory of multimarket contact competition. They estimate their model using data from multiple European countries for a blockbuster category of ethical drugs. They find that detailing elasticities are comparable across the United States, Germany, and Italy but are higher in the United Kingdom and France, suggesting a greater allocation of the detailing budget to the latter regions.

Fischer, Shankar, and Clement (2005) propose a market response model for entry timing across countries. Although they do not explicitly address allocation of marketing expenditures across countries, their results on marketing expenditures have implications for such allocation decisions. They find that a waterfall international entry strategy (entering markets sequentially) enhances marketing spending effectiveness. The normative implication for a brand that sequentially enters multiple markets or countries is that it should allocate greater spending to the later countries of entry than what would be appropriate based on market response in those countries if there were no prior entries in other countries.

Thus, although allocation across market or countries is a critical task, little practical guidance is available. The allocation criteria should go beyond country-specific factors, such as target market population, category growth, and profitability, to include cross-country effects that may be due to diffusion, market learning, and multimarket competition.

◆ ALLOCATION ACROSS CUSTOMERS AND CHANNELS

As organizations become more customer-centric, the allocation of resources by customers and customer segments is gaining greater importance than ever before. As companies increasingly offer their products through multiple channels, such as retail stores, the Web, and catalog or direct mail, and as more consumers buy them through different channels, the allocation of marketing efforts targeted at customers across channels is also becoming a critical issue for many marketers.

Models of marketing resource allocation across customers are primarily based on customer lifetime value (CLV). Venkatesan and Kumar (2004) identify low- and high-value customer segments on the basis of CLV and determine the optimal allocation of marketing resources to these segments. They maximize the following expression for CLV to determine x_{iml}, the optimal number of communication contacts to customer i in channel m in year l:

$$
(5) \qquad CLV_i = \sum_{y=1}^{T_i} \frac{CM_{iy}}{(1+r)^{y/f_i}} - \sum_{l=1}^{n} \frac{\sum_m c_{iml} x_{iml}}{(1+r)^{l-1}},
$$

where CM is predicted contribution margin, y is purchase occasion, r is discount rate, c is unit marketing cost, f is predicted purchase frequency, n is number of years to forecast, and T is predicted number of purchases until the end of the planning period. Applying this model to data from a large multinational computer hardware and software company, Venkatesan and Kumar find that the effect of marketing communication on CLV is nonlinear across channels and that marketers can improve profits by maximizing CLV.

Prior research has also examined the allocation between customer acquisition and retention (Reinartz, Thomas, and Kumar 2005) and between retention and reacquisition of lost customers (Thomas, Blattberg, and Fox 2004). (For a detailed review of allocation across customers in both the business-to-consumer and the business-to-business contexts, see Chapter 4.)

As the practice of allocation by customer segment has evolved, allocation across customer-channel segments has become the next key development in resource allocation practice (Kushwaha and Shankar 2007, 2008). A study by McKinsey & Company calls for developing resource allocation metrics across channels (Myers, Pickersgill, and Van Metre 2004). Neslin and colleagues (2006) emphasize the need to develop models for the allocation of marketing resources across channels.

Anderson, Lodish, and Weitz (1987) study the impact of variables associated with a financial portfolio model and the channel relationship on the selling time allocated by 71 independent sales agencies to the principals they represent. They find that the time (and resource) allocated to principals is consistent with an optimal microeconomic model, but channel relationship elements such as communication, participation, and feedback also influence resource allocation.

Kushwaha and Shankar (2008) propose an approach and model for optimal allocation of marketing efforts to each customer-channel segment. Although they do not incorporate participation and feedback, their approach is quite detailed, comprising marketing response models for each component of firm profit, purchase frequency, purchase quantity, product return propensity, and contribution margin. Their purchase frequency model is an extended beta geometric/negative binomial distribution model, purchase quantity and product return propensity is a conditional negative binomial distribution model, and contribution margin is a gamma–gamma model. The optimal marketing effort allocation to each customer-channel segment is a function of the model parameters for that segment. Kushwaha and Shankar estimate the models using customer-level purchase, cost, and promotional data from a large marketer of shoes and apparel accessories across the catalog, the store, and the Web and solve the optimization model in Excel using simulation.

The firm's objective function—total profits—is the sum of profits generated by each customer-channel segment of the firm. A firm that markets through K channels has K single-channel segments and one customer-channel segment of "multichannel" users. Let Π be the total profits of a firm over a given time horizon and Π_k be the profit of the kth customer-channel segment over the same horizon. Kushwaha and Shankar (2008) maximize Π_k for each customer-channel segment and Π for the firm across the customer-channel segments. The optimization equation is given by the following:

(6)
$$\max_{m_k} \sum_{k=1}^{K+1} \sum_{i=1}^{n_k} \left\{ \left[\mathrm{IPO}_{ik}\left(m_{ik}\right) - \mathrm{IRPO}_{ik} \right] \times \mathrm{NO}_{ik}\left(m_{ik}\right) \right.$$
$$\left. \times \overline{\mathrm{CM}}_{ik}\left(m_{ik}\right) - c_m m_{ik} \right\},$$

subject to $m_{ik} \geq 0$,

where m_{ik} is the number of marketing mailers sent to customer i from customer-channel segment k and is also the resource allocation variable and purchase frequency (NO_{ik}), purchase quantity per order (IPO_{ik}), and gross contribution margin ($\overline{\mathrm{CM}}_{ik}$) of customer i from customer-channel segment k are functions of the marketing efforts (m_{ik}) the firm expends toward that customer. The term IRPO_{ik} is product returns per order for customer i from customer-channel segment k and c_m and n_k are the unit cost of marketing and size of customer-channel segment k, respectively.

These results show that consumer response to the company's marketing efforts varies significantly across the customer-channel segments for the different profit components, purchase frequency, purchase quantity, and contribution margin. Figure 5.4 shows the dif-

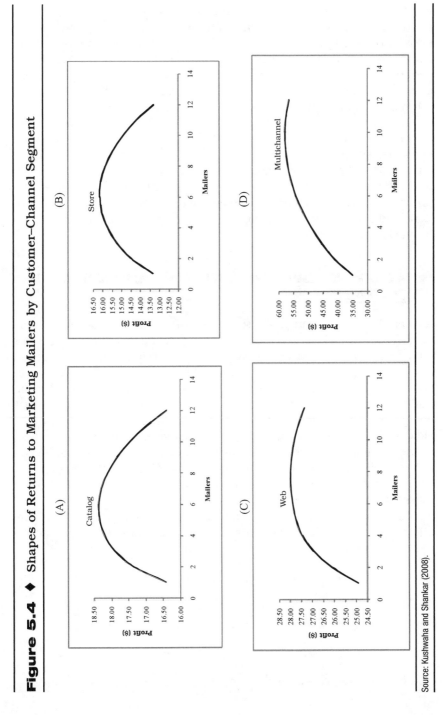

Source: Kushwaha and Shankar (2008).

ferential responsiveness across segments. Using a holdout sample analysis, Kushwaha and Shankar (2008) show that firm profits can be substantially improved by optimally reallocating marketing efforts across the different customer-channel segments. In their revised allocation, the multichannel segment exhibits the highest percentage growth in budget and profit, highlighting the high profit potential of the multichannel segment.

Overall, there are some useful insights into allocation by customers and channels. Firms should allocate more to customers and customer segments that have higher CLVs than others. Multichannel customer segments are most profitable, so an optimal allocation model based on the responsiveness of customer-channel segment by profit components, such as purchase frequency, quantity, contribution, and return propensity, can help marketers improve the returns to marketing efforts.

◆ ALLOCATION OVER THE PRODUCT LIFE CYCLE

As a product goes through different stages in the product life cycle, marketers' strategic allocation decisions heavily influence its growth. Prior empirical analyses offer conflicting evidence or guidelines on changes in advertising spending over the product life cycle. Lilien and Weinstein (1984) and Parsons (1975) suggest that firms should decrease advertising expenditures over the life cycle, while Winer (1979) suggests that companies should increase advertising spending over the life cycle. However, Farris and Buzzell (1979) find no evidence for the main effect of the product life cycle on advertising expenditures. These studies do not consider any interaction or moderating effects of the product life cycle, nor do they study the allocation between advertising and other marketing mix variables, such as sales force.

Shankar (2008) develops the following model to examine the effects of the product life cycle stages on a brand's strategic marketing allocation between advertising and the sales force.

$$(7) \qquad \ln \text{ME}_{it} = \alpha_{01t} + \sum_{k=2}^{K} \alpha_{0k} I_{ik} + \alpha_{1t} \ln \left(\text{PQ}_{i(t-1)} + 1 \right)$$

$$+ \alpha_{2t} \ln \left(\text{CONR}_{i(t-1)} + 1 \right) + \alpha_{3t} \text{MMC}_{i(t-1)} + \alpha_{4t} \text{NE}_{i(t-1)}$$

$$+ \alpha_{5t} \ln \text{DCOMPEX}_{i(t-1)} + \alpha_{6t} \ln \text{FCOMPEX}_{i(t-1)} + \alpha_{7} \ln \text{S}_{it}$$

$$+ \alpha_{8} \text{MLDR}_{i} + \alpha_{9} \ln \text{OME}_{it} + \varepsilon_{it}.$$

In this model,

- ME_{it} = strategic spending in the focal marketing variable (advertising or sales force) of brand i at time t;
- I_{ik} = a dummy variable denoting whether brand i is in category k;
- K = the total number of categories;
- PQ_{it} = the relative product quality of brand i at time t;
- $CONR_{it}$ = the market concentration in the market with brand i at time t;
- MMC_{it} = the multimarket contact of brand i with other brands in the market at time t;
- NE_{it} = a dummy variable denoting whether there was a new entry in the last six months preceding t in brand i's market;
- $DCOMPEX_{it}$ and $FCOMPEX_{it}$ = the total marketing expenditures of dominant and weak competitors, respectively, of brand i at time t;
- S_{it} = the sales of brand i at time t;
- $MLDR_i$ = a dummy variable denoting whether brand i is a leader in the focal marketing variable (advertising or sales force);
- OME_{it} = strategic spending in the other marketing variable (sales force or advertising) of brand i at time t; and
- ε_{it} = an error term assumed to be normal, independent with mean 0, and α_0–α_9 = the parameters.

Shankar (2008) allows the parameters to be moderated by the stage in the product life cycle. He estimates his model on data obtained from 29 brands in eight leading pharmaceutical categories over their life cycles. The results show that a brand's strategic marketing (pull vs. push, or emphasis on advertising vs. sales force expenditures) is moderated by its market position and the stage it is in the product life cycle. The results also show that dominant brands significantly shift their resource allocation toward a push strategy or sales force while moving from the growth to the mature stages of the product life cycle; in contrast, weak brands shift their allocations toward a pull strategy or advertising from the growth to the mature stages. Shankar also finds that the impact of the strategies of dominant and weak brands on each other is asymmetric and that dominant brands have a significant effect on weak-brand spending, but weak brands have no effect on dominant-brand spending. Furthermore, the results show that the effect of dominant brands on weak-brand spending differs from the early to the late stages of the product life cycle.

Shankar's (2008) data cover the largest therapeutic categories over long periods, making the analysis empirically generalizable to the pharmaceutical industry. Nevertheless, the data do not include R&D expenditures and do not cover other industries.

Taken together, the models offer some useful insights for effective resource allocation decisions over the product life cycle. A dominant (weak) brand shifts its strategic resource allocation toward a push (pull) strategy as it moves from the growth to the mature stages of the life cycle. Therefore, allocation to advertising relative to the sales force may decrease (increase) for dominant (weak) brands over their life in markets that are more elastic to sales force than advertising.

A summary of selected resource allocation models, the associated data, key findings, and limitations appears in Table 5.1. The models range from econometric models to optimization models to game-theoretic or other analytic models. The data cover a broad spectrum of industries, including CPGs, durables, pharmaceutical drugs, and industrial products. The key insights include optimal allocation based on competitively relative elasticities and several factors such as target population, category profitability, and growth potential. A key limitation of most models is that competitor responses—particularly, anticipated competitor actions—are not captured well. Furthermore, interaction effects among allocation variables are not often explicitly incorporated into the optimization approach.

◆ EMERGING AND FUTURE ISSUES

With the emergence and rapid growth of unmeasured and new media, the allocation of marketing resources to these avenues is becoming a challenging task for marketers of all products (Shankar and Hollinger 2007). Spending on unmeasured media includes expenditures on search engine marketing, Internet search ads, mobile media, social networking media, events, contests, in-store ads, and product placement. Although the proportion of the marketing budget allocated to such media is still low for many products, it is rising. For example, Nike's allocation of its U.S. advertising budget to unmeasured media increased from 45% in 1996 to 67% in 2006 (Story 2007).

Effective allocation models in the context of the new media require a deep understanding of the effectiveness of these media. Although improved data availability in the new media enables firms to measure their effectiveness more accurately than before, existing metrics are still in their infancy. For example, in the initial years of the Internet, marketing allocation to the Web was based primarily on "eyeballs" or site traffic. With the advent and growth of targeted search advertising pioneered by Google, click-through has become the key metric for allocating advertising dollars on the Web.

Table 5.1 ◆ Summary of Selected Marketing Resource Allocation Models

Article/Work	Model Type	Data	Key Findings/Guidelines	Key Limitations
Allocation Across Marketing and Product-Related Resources				
Erickson and Jacobson (1992)	Econometric model	99 firms from S&P database during 1972–1986	After firm-specific factors and the feedback between discretionary spending and profitability are controlled for, stock marketing spending is significantly lower, so firms should not overspend on R&D or marketing.	Residuals approximate unanticipated discretionary spending (R&D and marketing).
Bayus, Erickson, and Jacobson (2003)	Econometric model	Personal computers	Higher new product introductions and R&D spending are associated with lower marketing and advertising support.	Not generalizable to products in the mature and decline stages of the PLC. Results could be due to commoditization of product.
Allocation Across Products and Markets/Countries				
Lilien and Rao (1976)	Optimization model	Consumer product	The optimal number of outlets across geographic markets can be determined from an underlying S-shaped relationship between outlet share and market share.	Simulation-based without a closed-form solution. Not validated on empirical data.
Henderson (1998) (The BCG matrix)	Conceptual model	N.A.	Milk the cash cows and feed question marks to upgrade them into stars if needed. Stars self-finance themselves. Get rid of dogs, unless they are strategic complements or have substantial exit barriers.	Too simplistic dimensions. Assumes profits correlated with relative market shares. Assumes a static view of the business universe.

Table 5.1 ◆ Continued

Article/Work	Model Type	Data	Key Findings/Guidelines	Key Limitations
Allocation Across Products and Markets/Countries (continued)				
Chintagunta and Desiraju (2005)	Econometric (structural, empirical industrial organization) model	Pharmaceuticals	Detailing elasticities are comparable across U.S., Germany, and Italy, but are higher in U.K. and France, suggesting greater allocation of detailing budget to U.K. and France.	Not an explicitly normative model of resource allocation across countries.
Fischer, Shankar, and Clement (2005)	Econometric model	Pharmaceuticals	Marketing efficacy is higher in later countries of entry if firms follow a waterfall strategy, so firms should allocate more in later countries than that suggested by independent country response behavior.	Not an explicitly normative model of resource allocation across countries.
Marketing Mix Allocation and Allocation over the Product Life Cycle (PLC)				
Lilien (1979)	Econometric (logit and linear regression) models	ADVISOR2 survey data from 22 companies for 131 products	Allocation to sales force determined by firm size, order size, stage in the product life cycle, product complexity, and purchase frequency.	Inappropriate for new products, narrow sample composition, U.S.-centric data.
Shankar (1997)	Analytical and econometric (game-theoretic and empirical industrial organization) model	A large drug product category	Brands should allocate resources between advertising and sales force in the ration of competitive relative elasticities.	Decoupled response function.

Table 5.1 ♦ Continued

Article/Work	Model Type	Data	Key Findings/Guidelines	Key Limitations
Marketing Mix Allocation and Allocation over the Product Life Cycle (PLC) (continued)				
Sethuraman and Tellis (1991)	Analytical and econometric model	Nondurable and durable goods	Promotions (price discounts) are more profitable than advertising for mature products, so allocate more to promotions.	Other marketing variables not considered. Interaction effect ignored.
Neslin, Powell, and Stone (1995)	Analytical model	N.A.	Advertising and trade promotion expenditures are substitutes and balance each other.	No empirical evidence.
Naik, Raman, and Winer (2005)	Optimization (differential game) model with continuous-discrete estimation method	Detergents	Advertising and promotion have significant interaction effects. Large brands underadvertise and overpromote. Small brands underadvertise and overpromote.	Model ignores category sales changes; ignores carryover effects; other mix variables omitted; role of retailer absent.
Shankar (2008)	Econometric (market response) model	Pharmaceuticals	Marketing expenditures and moderated by the stage in the PLC. Dominant brands shift allocation of sales force over the PLC.	R&D decision not considered.
Allocation Across Customers and Channels				
Venkatesan and Kumar (2004)	Optimization model at customer-cohort level	B2B customer data from a multinational computer hardware and software firm	Optimization based on CLV yields improved profits relative to other optimization approaches.	Competitor responses not included in the model; indirectly relate costs and margins to CRM efforts.

Table 5.1 ♦ Continued

Article/Work	Model Type	Data	Key Findings/Guidelines	Key Limitations
Allocation Across Customers and Channels (continued)				
Anderson, Lodish, and Weitz (1987)	Econometric (S-shaped effort allocation) model; factor analysis of survey responses	Survey data from 95 firms belonging to Electronic Representatives Association (ERA)	Allocation of time by sales agencies to principal consistent with micro-economic model, but is also affected by communication, participation, and feedback.	Self-reporting bias; common method variance; key informant bias; one industry view.
Kushwaha and Shankar (2008)	Optimization model decomposed into purchases frequency, quantity, and margin models	Shoes and accessories	The model produces a 32% increase in total profits in a holdout sample. Multi-channel customers are most responsive to marketing mailers.	Models applied in only one industry.

Marketers, however, are still searching for a more appropriate measure because click-through still suffers from limitations, such as the inability to control for click-fraud.

The core principle of allocating resources in proportion to their competitively relative elasticities is no different in this context than it is in the context of traditional media, the only exception being that the key metrics used for measuring customer responsiveness to marketing in these media are different from those in traditional media. As these metrics evolve, the resource allocation models will become more specific to the media.

As we move forward, resource allocation contexts and elements will likely become more complex. Although the basic principles of resource allocation and fundamental underpinnings will likely stay the same, the actual allocation rules will be based more on simulation than before. In many cases, closed-form analytical expressions for optimal resource allocation decisions may not be available, so managers will need to rely more on simulations for deriving the optimal decisions. Such simulations will not be as onerous a task as in the past, given the availability of richer data and greater computing power than before. In the future, managers will be more likely to use simulators and decision support systems for resource allocation than they did in the past.

What should the future research priorities with regard to marketing resource allocation be? First, we need to develop resource allocation models that are based on the relationship between marketing spending and company or shareholder value rather than on the link between marketing expenditures and profits alone. Second, future resource allocation models should incorporate different scenarios of anticipated competitor responses in deriving optimal allocation rules. Third, there should be greater research on allocation of resources to the new media. Fourth, additional research is needed on the linkages between different types and levels of allocation decisions.

Existing research allocation models focus on a single allocation type or level or context (e.g., marketing vs. sales force allocation, allocation across products) in isolation. Because many resource allocation decisions are interdependent, we need models that simultaneously optimize across different types of decisions. For example, a model that simultaneously optimizes allocation between R&D and marketing and within the marketing mix could offer more effective and precise allocation rules. Such models would likely be complex and simulation based. Finally, research on the convergence of insights from the different types of allocation models is desirable.

◆ Conclusion

As the allocation of marketing resources continues to be a critical strategic priority for CMOs and other marketing executives worldwide, the application of existing models of strategic allocation and the emergence of new models are gaining importance. Strategic allocation of resources includes those between marketing and nonmarketing (e.g., R&D) variables; across marketing mix, products, markets, countries, customers, and channels; and over the product life cycle. Different models are available for these decisions. The core principle of allocation in these models is based on the relative responsiveness or elasticity of the outcome variable (e.g., sales, profits) to change in the allocation elements (e.g., marketing vs. R&D, products, and channels). The relative elasticity is driven by factors such as the industry, company size, strengths and weaknesses, and stage in the product life cycle.

Although these models offer important guidance to managers, considerable potential exists for improved models of resource allocation that can incorporate greater complexity, interactions among variables, and anticipated competitor responses. To offer improved managerial guidance, future models of resource allocation should address issues such as the relationship of spending with shareholder value, incorporation of future competitor responses, spending on new media, and linkages between different types and levels of allocation.

◆ Notes

1. This example is drawn from Corstjens and Merrihue's (2003) work.
2. We do not address the issue of overall optimal budget determination, though the allocation and overall budget decisions may be related (Lodish et al. 1988; Mantrala, Sinha, and Zoltners 1992).

◆ References

Anderson, Erin, Leonard M. Lodish, and Barton A. Weitz (1987), "Resource Allocation Behavior in Conventional Channels," *Journal of Marketing Research*, 25 (February), 85–97.

Bayus, Barry L., Gary Erickson, and Robert Jacobson (2003), "The Financial Rewards of New Product Introduction in the Personal Computers Industry," *Management Science*, 49 (2), 197–211.

Chintagunta, Pradeep K. and Ramarao Desiraju (2005), "Strategic Pricing and Detailing Behavior in International Markets," *Marketing Science*, 24 (1), 67–80.

CMO Council (2007), *CMO Council 07 Outlook Report*, (accessed December 10, 2007), [available at http://www.cmocouncil.org].

Corstjens, Marcel and Jeffrey Merrihue (2003), "Optimal Marketing," *Harvard Business Review*, (October), 114–21.

Dekimpe, Marnik G. and Dominique M. Hanssens (1999), "Sustained Spending and Persistent Response: A New Look at Long-Term Marketing Profitability," *Journal of Marketing Research*, 36 (November), 397–412.

Dorfman, Robert and Peter O. Steiner (1954), "Optimal Advertising and Optimal Quality," *American Economic Review*, 44 (5), 826–36.

Elsner, Ralf, Manfred Krafft, and Arnd Huchzermeier (2004), "Optimizing Rhenania's Direct Marketing Business Through Dynamic Multilevel Modeling (DMLM) in a Multicatalog-Brand Environment," *Marketing Science*, 23 (2), 192–206.

Erickson, Gary and Robert Jacobson (1992), "Gaining Comparative Advantage Through Discretionary Expenditures: Returns to R&D and Advertising," *Management Science*, 38 (9), 1264–79.

Farris, Paul and Robert Buzzell (1979), "Why Advertising and Promotional Costs Vary: Some Cross-Sectional Analyses," *Journal of Marketing*, 43 (Autumn), 112–22.

Fischer, Marc, Venkatesh Shankar, and Michel Clement (2005), "Can a Late Mover Use International Market Entry Strategy to Challenge the Pioneer?" MSI Report No. 05-004, Marketing Science Institute.

Gatignon, Hubert (1993), "Marketing Mix Models," in *Handbook in Operations Research and Management Science: Marketing*, J. Eliashberg and Gary L. Lilien, eds. Amsterdam: Elsevier Science, 697–728.

Henderson, Bruce (1998), "The Product Portfolio," in *Perspectives on Strategy from the Boston Consulting Group*, Carl W. Stern and George Stalk Jr., eds. Boston: BCG Publications.

IMS Health (2006), *IMS Retail Drug Monitor*, (December), (accessed March 6, 2008), [available at http://www.imshealth.com/ims/portal/front/indexC/ 0,2773,6599_77685579_0,00.html].

Kerin, Roger A., Vijay Mahajan, and P. Rajan Varadarajan (1990), *Contemporary Perspectives on Strategic Market Planning*. Boston: Allyn & Bacon.

Kushwaha, Tarun and Venkatesh Shankar (2007), "Single Channel vs. Multichannel Customers: Determinants and Value to Retailers," working paper, Mays Business School, Texas A&M University.

——— and ——— (2008), "Optimal Allocation of Marketing Efforts by Customer-Channel Segment," working paper, Mays Business School, Texas A&M University.

Lilien, Gary L. (1979), "Advisor 2: Modeling the Marketing Mix Decision for Industrial Products," *Management Science*, 25 (2), 191–204.

——— and Ambar G. Rao (1976), "A Model for Allocating Retail Outlet Building Resources Across Market Areas," *Operations Research*, 24 (1), 1–14.

——— and David Weinstein (1984), "An International Comparison of the Determinants of Industrial Marketing Expenditures," *Journal of Marketing*, 48 (Winter), 46–53.

Little, John D.C. (1970), "Models and Managers: The Concept of Decision Calculus," *Management Science*, 16 (8), B466–B484.

Lodish, Leonard M. (1971), "CALLPLAN: An Interactive Salesman's Call Planning System," *Management Science*, 18 (12), 25–40.

———, E. Curtis, M. Ness, and M.K. Simpson (1988), "Sales Force Sizing and Deployment Using a Decision Calculus Model at Syntex Laboratories," *Interfaces*, 18 (January–February), 5–20.

Mantrala, Murali, K. (2002), "Allocating Marketing Resources," in *Handbook of Marketing*, Barton A. Weitz and Robin Wensely, eds. Thousand Oaks, CA: Sage Publications, 409–435.

———, Prabhakant Sinha, and Andris A. Zoltners (1992), "Impact of Resource Allocation Rules on Marketing Investment-Level Decisions and Profitability," *Journal of Marketing Research*, 29 (May), 162–75.

Myers, Joseph B., Andrew D. Pickersgill, and Evan S. Van Metre (2004), "Steering Customers to the Right Channels," *McKinsey Quarterly*, 4 (December 7), 36–48.

Naik, Prasad A., Kalyan Raman, and Russell S. Winer (2005), "Planning Marketing-Mix Strategies in the Presence of Interaction Effects," *Marketing Science*, 24 (1), 25–34.

Neff, Jack (2004), "P&G, Clorox Discover Modeling: Marketing Mix Analytics Gain New Proponents," *Advertising Age*, (March 29), 10.

Neslin, Scott A., D. Grewal, R. Leghorn, V. Shankar, M.L. Teerling, J.S. Thomas, and P.C. Verhoef (2006), "Challenges and Opportunities in Multichannel Management," *Journal of Service Research*, 9 (2), 95–113.

———, Stephen G. Powell, and Linda Schneider Stone (1995), "The Effects of Retailer and Consumer Response on Optimal Manufacturer and Trade Promotion Strategies," *Management Science*, 41 (5), 749–66.

Parsons, Leonard J. (1975), "The Product Life Cycle and Time Varying Advertising Elasticities," *Journal of Marketing Research*, 12 (November), 476–80.

PhRMA (2007), *Pharmaceutical Industry Profile 2007*, (March), (accessed February 21, 2008), [available at http://www.phrma.org/files/Profile%202007.pdf].

Rangaswamy, Arvind and Lakshman Krishnamurthi (1991), "Response Function Estimation Using the Equity Estimator," *Journal of Marketing Research*, 28 (February), 72–83.

———, Prabhakant Sinha, and Andris Zoltners (1990), "An Integrated Model-Based Approach for Sales Force Structuring," *Marketing Science*, 9 (4), 279–98.

Reinartz, Werner, Jacquelyn S. Thomas, and V. Kumar (2005), "Balancing Acquisition and Retention Resources to Maximize Customer Profitability," *Journal of Marketing*, 69 (January), 63–79.

Richardson, Robert J. (2004), "A Marketing Resource Allocation Model," *Journal of Business & Economic Studies*, 10 (1), 43–53.

Sethuraman, Raj and Gerard J. Tellis (1991), "An Analysis of the Tradeoff Between Advertising and Price Discounting," *Journal of Marketing Research*, 27 (May), 160–74.

Shankar, Venkatesh (1997), "Pioneers' Marketing Mix Reactions to Entry in Different Competitive Games Structures: Theoretical Analysis and Empirical Illustration," *Marketing Science,* 16 (4), 271–93.

——— (2006), "Proactive and Reactive Product Line Strategies: Asymmetries Between Market Leaders and Followers," *Management Science,* 52 (2), 276–92.

——— (2008), "The Role of Product Life Cycle and Market Dominance in Marketing Expenditures of Products," working paper, Mays Business School, Texas A&M University.

——— and Marie Hollinger (2007), "Online and Mobile Advertising: Current Scenario, Emerging Trends, and Future Directions," MSI Report No. 07-206, Marketing Science Institute.

Story, Louise (2007), "The New Advertising Outlet: Your Life," *The New York Times,* (October 14), (accessed March 6, 2008), [available at http://www.nytimes.com/2007/10/14/business/media/14ad.html?_r=1&oref=slogin].

Thomas, Jacquelyn, Robert C. Blattberg, and Edward Fox (2004), "Recapturing Lost Customers," *Journal of Marketing Research,* 41 (February), 31–45.

Tode, Chantal (2007), "Procter & Gamble Marketing Looks to Internet," *DMNews,* (May 7), (accessed March 6, 2008), [available at http://www.dmnews.com/Procter—Gamble-marketing-looks-to-Internet/article/95420/].

Venkatesan, Rajkumar and V. Kumar (2004), "A Customer Lifetime Value Framework for Customer Selection and Resource Allocation Strategy," *Journal of Marketing,* 68 (October), 106–126.

Winer, Russell S. (1979), "An Analysis of the Time-Varying Effects of Advertising: The Case of Lydia Pynkam," *Journal of Business,* 52 (4), 563–76.

AFTERWORD

TAKING STOCK

In *Competing on Analytics: The New Science of Winning*, Davenport and Harris (2007) argue that the intelligent use of data-collection technology and the development and application of sophisticated statistical and modeling techniques represent a source of competitive advantage for companies. In a similar vein, the perspectives and practices detailed in this volume demonstrate that advances in marketing mix resource allocation and planning analytics can offer valuable insights into the linkage among marketing investments, market response, and financial metrics.

As the first product of the American Marketing Association Knowledge Coalition's effort to address contemporary issues facing senior marketing executives and marketing research professionals, *Marketing Mix Decisions: New Perspectives and Practices* is not intended to provide a definitive statement on marketing mix resource allocation and planning. Rather, this volume attempts to initiate dialogue within and between the practitioner and academic communities on the shortages and surpluses in the state of knowledge and practice, with attention given to new media.

In the introduction to this book, three areas of concern were mentioned. They include modest budgetary and organizational support for media experimentation, limited business experience with and talent necessary to apply marketing analytics to new media, and insufficient metrics and marketing analytics to measure the efficiency and effectiveness of new media alongside traditional media. These concerns are not mutually exclusive. In looking ahead, marketers will need to address all three areas—beginning with whichever one they believe is most critical—to develop (or sustain) a winning approach to resource allocation and planning for their marketing programs.

◆ Gaining Top Management Support

Senior marketing executives and marketing research professionals will need to gain the confidence and support of their company's chief financial officer before a chief executive officer will authorize any significant increase in marketing investment for media experimentation and recruitment of analytical talent (LaPointe 2007). This confidence (and subsequent support) will come only from demonstrable success in applying analytical and modeling techniques to all marketing programs, as well as identifying marketing metrics that can be linked empirically to financial results.

In short, senior marketing executives frequently encounter a frustrating "catch-22" situation, in which budgetary support for experimentation and analytics is dependent on documented success in their use, which in turn is based on prior support and investment in analytical and modeling techniques. Without the latter, the former is unlikely, and a stalemate results. It is hoped that the research applications and results highlighted in this volume will serve as a constructive beginning for dialogue in the corporate executive suite. In particular, the case studies that V. Kumar presents in "Optimal Allocation of Marketing Mix Resources: B2C and B2B Case Studies" (Chapter 4) offer two detailed examples that demonstrate success in applying analytical and modeling techniques; these are important proof points on the road to credibility.

◆ Building an Analytical Marketing Infrastructure and Culture

The rapid evolution of marketing mix models has not necessarily translated to rapid adoption by companies. Senior marketing executives continue to be hamstrung by organizational and cultural barriers, which fuels their own indecision about which initiatives to fund, often with limited discretionary dollars, and the methods by which to measure their progress. In many cases, marketers have yet to adjust their operations to support new media channels and implement new processes and techniques for allocating marketing resources and measuring results.

In looking ahead, companies will need to consider reorganizing their internal structures to house a Center of Excellence that integrates (or at least has access to) all customer data that reside in isolated databases across the organization and that employs the talent to interpret and apply state-of-the-art analytical and modeling techniques to these data. The efforts of the IBM Market Intelligence Center of Excellence that Todd Powers and Anil Menon describe in "Practical Measurement of Advertising Impact: The IBM Experience" (Chapter 3) demonstrate the benefits of such an organizational structure.

◆ ACCOUNTABILITY IN MEASUREMENT AND MANAGEMENT

The adage "If you can't measure it, you can't manage it" has direct bearing on marketing mix resource allocation and planning analysis in the broader context of marketing accountability. Indeed, a recent survey conducted on behalf of the Association of National Advertisers (2007) indicates that more than half of senior marketing executives polled remain dissatisfied with the progress they have made toward formalizing marketing accountability programs with their companies. Gordon Wyner's article, titled "Marketing Effectiveness: Practical Approaches to Measurement and Management" (Chapter 2), offers insightful guidance on formulating an approach to achieving accountability in measurement and management.

Building a culture of accountability begins by taking stock of your organizational knowledge. Senior marketing executives and marketing research professionals need to be cognizant of what they know, and what they don't know, in the domain of marketing mix resource allocation and planning. Otherwise, considerable time, intellectual energy, and dollars can be misdirected. Donald Rumsfeld, the former U.S. secretary of defense, provides an apt characterization of the challenge of cataloging knowledge:

> There are known knowns; there are things we know we know. We also know there are unknowns; that is to say, we know there are some things we do not know. But there are also unknown unknowns—the ones we don't know we don't know. (in Eisenberg and Fisher 2007, p. 142)

The overviews in this volume prepared by Sunil Gupta and Thomas Steenburgh in "Allocating Marketing Resources" (Chapter 1) and Venkatesh Shankar in "Strategic Allocation of Marketing Resources:

Methods and Insights" (Chapter 5) carefully describe "known knowns," alert the reader to what we "know are unknowns," and speculate about the realm of "unknown unknowns" in the science and practice of marketing mix resource allocation and planning.

Adding more focus and discipline around the knowns and the unknowns of marketing budgeting and planning will always be a significant challenge; there is no silver bullet for determining the optimal mix. However, practitioners and scholars who are willing to share their learnings and collaborate closely on new methodologies and techniques will continue to shed light on new approaches for improving both the strategy and the process of marketing resource allocation and planning. And from that, we all stand to benefit.

◆ REFERENCES

Association of National Advertisers (2007), "AMA/MMA Marketing Accountability Study Finds Need for Greater Alignment Between Marketing and Finance," press release, (September 5).

Davenport, Thomas H. and Jeanne G. Harris (2007), Competing on Analytics: *The New Science of Winning.* Boston: Harvard Business School Press.

Eisenberg, Evan and Jeffrey Fisher (2007), "Essay," *Time,* (January 29), 142.

LaPointe, Pat (2007), "Building Blocks," *Marketing Management,* 16 (May–June), 18–25.

INDEX

Return on investment (ROI) analysis
of advertising, 43, 96
of branding impact, 19, 115
conversion of elasticities into, 10
of direct-to-consumer advertising, 19–20
of marketing activities, 117–18
of marketing instruments, 17, 18
of marketing mix variables, 131, 132
resources for, 54
Revenue
distribution of, 131
effect of ad exposure on, 40
tie into advertising campaigns, 104–6
Risk, assessing, 46
Rock Bottom Brewery, 13

S
Sales force
allocation between advertising and, 161–63
decision calculus in planning for, 26–27
Sales promotion, allocation between advertising and, 163–65
Sales-response model, 112
Sales revenue, effect of ad exposure on, 40
Sampling, 71, 124
experience, 71
occasion-based, 71
Samsung Electronics, 155, 157
Scanner data, 35n1
Self-reports, 70–71
Sentence-completion exercises, 81
Shankar, Venkatesh, 112
Share of wallet (SOW), 136–37
Short run, long run versus, 43
Silo mentality, 68–69
Simulations, 11, 21
limitations of, 11
SKUs, 74–75, 122–23
Social networking, 3, 7, 12
Spillover effects, 4
Split-cable experiments, 8, 35n4
S-shaped advertising response function, 16
Standard regression analysis, 17
Stars, 166, 167
Steenburgh, Thomas, 1

Strategic allocation of marketing, product-related resources and, 157–66
Strategic allocation of marketing resources, 154–80
Strategic decision making, 157
Strategic intent, clarifying, 51, 52
Structural equation modeling (SEM), 100, 104
Systematic testing process, 56, 58

T
Telephone communication, 135
Television advertising, 16, 43, 55, 56, 113, 123–24
halo effect of, 128
print advertising impact on effectiveness of, 128–29, 130
Television total advertising rating point (TARP) values, 124, 126
Territorial differences, 131
Test-and-control samples, 8
3 × 3 matrix, 5
Times-series regression model, 59
Top-down approaches
as choice for big ad spenders, 74
marketing mix modeling as, 58–64
on market performance, 39
Top-down budgets, xi
Touch-point measurement, 70
Trading event meetings, 134
Traditional metrics, performance of, versus customer lifetime value (CLV) metric, 139
Transition probabilities, Bayesian procedure in estimating, 32
Translation, 54
Tremor, 12
Tremor Teen, 12

U
Unilever, 12
United Airlines, 26
Up-front alignment process, 56

V
V8 vegetable juice, 16
Value of customers, understanding, 39
Video games, 3, 12
Virtual worlds, 3, 12
Vocalpoint, 12, 13

W

Web-based communication, 135
Web presence, 152
Web sites, 12
Weighted distributions, 123
Welch, Greg, xii
"What-if" analysis, 11, 20–23
Willingness-to-pay measure, 30
Word-of-mouth marketing (WOM), 3, 12–14

effectiveness of communication, 12–14
Wyner, Gordon, 39–40

Y

Young, Charles E., 87
YouTube, 12

Z

Zip codes, information in, 29